MARY WEBB
HER LIFE AND WORK

THE WORKS OF MARY WEBB

MARY WEBB (GLADYS MARY MEREDITH)
IN HER EARLY 'TEENS.

THOMAS MOULT

*

MARY WEBB:
HER LIFE AND WORK

LONDON
JONATHAN CAPE 30 BEDFORD SQUARE

FIRST PUBLISHED IN MCMXXXII

JONATHAN CAPE LTD. 30 BEDFORD SQUARE LONDON
& 91 WELLINGTON STREET WEST, TORONTO

PRINTED IN GREAT BRITAIN BY
BUTLER & TANNER LTD
FROME

Contents

List of Illustrations

Note

In making this attempt at an authorized biography and a literary estimate I have had the great privilege of the help of Mary Webb's family and friends, who placed themselves freely at my service. I wish to express my thanks to them, and especially to her husband, Mr. H. B. L. Webb, who has kindly read the book in proof; her brother, Captain Douglas Meredith, M.C.; and her lifelong friend, Miss E. M. Lory. For my use of passages from the writings of Mary Webb, which are published by Mr. Jonathan Cape, I make full acknowledgment.

T. M.

MARY WEBB

★

One of the best living writers.

SIR JAMES BARRIE

Mary Webb is a genius.

REBECCA WEST

I am glad I was in time to send her a few words of appreciation.

RT. HON. STANLEY BALDWIN

Much of the noble work of Mary Webb might be called the prose poems of a Shropshire Lass.

G. K. CHESTERTON

Few writers indeed have left behind them so rich a posthumous gift.

WALTER DE LA MARE

Mary Webb had that always fascinating quality of genius — imaginative energy. It is a quality so precious that when an author possesses it the waves of criticism beat against his work in vain.

ROBERT LYND

9

No one of our day has a greater power of evoking natural magic. Mary Webb need fear no comparison with any writer who has attempted to capture the soul of nature in words and to 'tease us out of thought' by glimpses into an ancient inheritance.

JOHN BUCHAN

She has a style of exquisite beauty, which yet has both force and restraint, simplicity and subtlety: she has fancy and wit, delicious humour and pathos. She has, in short, genius.

EDWIN PUGH

Her work is alive with the fiery genius of sympathy, pity, and awe. . . . It is not too much to say that in her writings fiction becomes a branch of poetry – a flowering branch that will still give pleasure for many years to come.

ROBERT LYND

Mary Webb's sensibility is so acute and her power over words so sure and swift that one who reads some passages in Whitehall has almost the physical sense of being in Shropshire cornfields.

RT. HON. STANLEY BALDWIN

FROM the summit of a Shropshire hill a woman used to gaze out upon the stupendous panorama of mountains and valleys that followed the sky, east to west, so spaciously that its distant rim formed the horizon of five counties. It was as if she stood at the extreme end of a narrow peninsula. The four winds would blow through her uncovered hair, and the rising and falling plains and ranges, dimly blue and green and golden, swept like a broad encircling sea against the heathery slopes, far below her feet. Even if she wheeled herself completely round, the continuous picture she beheld was only broken for an instant by the width of the plateau on which she lingered.

Silence and solitude were about her, but she was content, for she had sought them. Most of her days, just then, were silent and solitary, except for one companion who shared the home they had made together on this high hill overlooking a landscape seemingly empty of life, so that a tiny puff of smoke where a railway train crept across the middle distance, or a hare flashing soundlessly through the near-by bracken, became a tremendous trifle. Only a few steps away was a little gate that had swung behind her as she came forward to the unfenced edge of these heathery slopes. It shut upon a tangled, lovely wilderness of garden, and along the rough garden-path, a cottage, single-storied, lately built of brick and tile. Day by day she stepped over her threshold and stood looking forth upon that eternal panorama of 'dimpled lands and gaunt purple steeps'; and her demeanour suggested an intensity and fascination hardly to be understood, unless the observer knew that it was also the panorama of her own life.

. . . Of her own life, from the very beginning. Yonder to the north-east, under a hill that from the angle of her view appeared to rise sharply, she could see, without moving, a coloured haze of farms and clustering houses, ten miles distant, where she was born. Wheeling eastward she saw a rugged low range against the sky that held the village in which she spent half her eager girlhood. Beyond the horizon and the brooding clouds, hundreds of miles away, was London. . . . But she would not have dwelt over-much on London in the panorama of her years, except as the place where genius is crowned, and men and women do homage. . . . Southward the dales, woods, and pastures were rich for her with girlish and young womanly recollections – of 'yellow harvests, of axes barking in the forest, of rickyards, and spacious kitchens lit by the Christmas faggot'; of care-free day-long rambles that left her white with dust and braced by parching sunshine or by wild and buffeting storms from which she never shrank, because all her life, frail though she was, she had met all weathers face to face. Far westward, drawn by another jagged hill, her eyes could mark a spot in which she once lived as a woman, and had been happy and had suffered. . . . And so back to the north, where, half-hidden by the shoulder of the plateau, brooded the only town she loved, whose half-timbered houses and quaint crooked streets and lanes and market-square were steeped with memories of old laughter and tears, and life and death. For there the last home stood, that she had shared with her father and mother, her sisters and brothers; there she had married and there she began the work that became her life's purpose, the dream and the deed.

And now she was still among her 'enchanted hills,' alone with her own story. All this that

her gaze could span as she turned to the north-
east, where the Wrekin rose afar, and Leighton
village lay below it; as she turned slowly south,
seeing Wenlock Edge and the Church Stretton
hills, and then westward, seeing Pontesbury
and the Stiper Stones; and north again, catching
a glimpse of the half-visible Shrewsbury town —
all this was gradually becoming, not a world outside, across blue distances, but her own created
world. She was re-making it in her poetry
and prose — in her books whose writing was 'a
sweetness in much bitter,' books that had the
fragrance and homeliness of the place even in
their names — *The Golden Arrow, Gone to Earth,
The House in Dormer Forest, Seven for a Secret,
Precious Bane.* . . .

Her own name was Mary Webb, and she
stood on Lyth Hill, near Shrewsbury. No
wonder she lingered there, day by day, during
the matured years of her work and her life,
for she was being vouchsafed an experience
unshared by any but a few beings in an era
of uprootings from the soil and scatterings to
the earth's four corners, so that hardly anyone lives out his days in the house at which he
was given birth. It was the panorama of her
whole life that spread before her.

14

CHAPTER ONE

Early Days – mainly in a 'Rip Van Winkle of a Borough'

I

MARY WEBB was born on March 25th, 1881, at Leighton, a Shropshire village named after Tihel de Lahtune, Lord of the Manor in the reign of Henry the First. She was the first child of George Edward and Sarah Alice Meredith, and was christened Gladys Mary. Her grandparents were no longer living, her father having married comparatively late in life. He was thirty-nine years old when he, a man of Welsh descent though with an English birthplace, brought the daughter of an Edinburgh physician to that imposing Victorian house of gables and tall chimneys. Mr. Meredith's father and grandfather had been in turn the Vicar of Leighton Parish Church, where the child Gladys Mary was christened. Her uncle too was a clergyman, but to assume any exceptional atmosphere of piety in that Leighton household would not be correct, unless 'piety' were interpreted in the wide sense of culture and humanity.

'I do not recall my father as of the parson type,' writes Captain Douglas Meredith, a younger son. 'True, we had family prayers each morning and evening, but although he loved his books, especially the Waverley Novels, he was by no means exclusively studious. He used to sketch and paint; he was an enthusiastic gardener; and what with one thing and another he spent a large part of his time out of doors. We were the sons and daughters of country house people.'

George Edward Meredith was also a poet on occasion. When his children's birthdays came round, he conveyed his greetings in verse. Among Mary Webb's poems there is one entitled 'Treasures' that she dedicated to 'G. E. M.,' and it memorializes her father's main characteristics:

'These are my treasures: just a word, a look,
A chiming sentence from his favourite book,
A large, blue, scented blossom that he found
And plucked for me in some enchanted ground,
A joy he planned for us, a verse he made
Upon a birthday, the increasing shade
Of trees he planted by the waterside,
The echo of a laugh, his tender pride

16

In those he loved, his hand upon my hair,
The dear voice lifted in his evening prayer.'

A fragment of the 'verse he made upon a birthday' describes how 'dim among the heather harebells grow between.' He was gay in his verse, as well as serious. The following lines, which will serve to illustrate how wittily gay he could be, are taken from a poetical message addressed to a guest of the household who had been seized with indisposition during her stay:

'What was it laid its cruel grip
   Upon her back, and thigh, and hip;
And spoiled the pleasure of her trip?
    Lumbago!

     *   *   *

'The singer of this little song
   Hopes that his guest will soon be strong,
And that the back-fiend will ere long
    Away go!!!'

George Edward Meredith was quick to appreciate the quaintness and comicality of village life. He used to repeat the saying of an old tailor who undertook to repair a suit of his clothes and promised: 'Well, Maister

Meredith, the Lord willing you shall have it on Saturday. You shall have it on Monday whether or no.' That suit of clothes must have been his Sunday best, for on weekdays he put one on that he never troubled to have mended. There is in existence a faded photograph of Mr. Meredith in the garden, with his eldest daughter, not yet in her 'teens, standing at his side. He is leaning on a spade. The clothes he is wearing are certainly not his Sunday best; they must have belonged to another story he used to chuckle over, although it counted against himself. A tramp called out to the shabby-looking man in the garden at Leighton, 'What's the maister like up at the house yonder?' Mr. Meredith's reply was: 'I don't know. You'd better go and see.'

He is remembered as a popular figure in the surrounding countryside. He was often to be encountered on the roads with his dogs; he kept greyhounds and a pack of beagles. He had a poultry-farm, and would chat by the hour with the villagers about fowls and dogs. His profession has been described as that of a schoolmaster, but this is wrong; he was only a schoolmaster in the sense that he took pupils and prepared them for Sandhurst and the universities. A 'varsity man himself, he had a rich store of college reminiscences, including one that concerned three inseparable old dons who were known as 'The World, the Flesh, and the Devil.' The third of them, 'the Devil', had a daughter. Once she beheld them approaching along the street, and she remarked to her companions: 'Here come the World, the Flesh, and Papa.'

II

Llewellyn King of Wales is supposed to have been a remote ancestor of the Merediths, for although England had been their birthplace for four generations there is a spot in Wales called by the same name that once belonged to the family. Not that Gladys Mary Meredith's father, genial, unassuming, without pride, ever troubled about family connections. There were so many things he never troubled about. 'Mr. Meredith,' a friend of the family remembers, 'used to meet me at the Shrewsbury railway station when I went to stay with them, but he was always late!'

Mrs. Meredith, on the other hand, would have cherished all such details of ancestry with open pride. Sarah Alice Scott, as she was before her marriage, claimed kinship with Sir Walter Scott, but the connection is too vague to be traced. She was greatly admired and regarded affectionately by those who knew the Merediths. She seems to have given the impression of a noble-minded woman who wore the cloak of strict piety more easily than her husband would have done. The idea of duty, justice, and honour was paramount in her lengthy life. She liked to keep her dearest possessions in her own room rather than spread them through the house. This pathetic habit is lovingly noted by Mary Webb in a poem 'To Mother, Christmas 1920':

'Within the doorway of your room to-night
I stood, and saw your little treasures all
Set out beneath the golden candle light
While silver chimes haunted the evenfall.
. . . Childish presents, bought with grave delight,
For many an ancient Christmas festival.'

Mrs. Meredith was an earnest cultivator of flowers. And although she spent less time out of doors with her children than their father did, it is a very motherly lady who may be seen in photographs of her, seated in the garden, diligently trimming dahlias or looking thoughtfully out from a trellis of roses. She survived her husband by sixteen years. At his funeral in 1909 the presiding clergyman paid a tribute to his many virtues:

'Devout, unselfish, ever ready to give his help, kindly, open-handed, humble-minded almost to a fault, and with a cheery word of greeting for all, he never failed to create in those with whom he came into contact a feeling that they were the better for his friendship. The one thing which preyed on his mind was a feeling that he was doing less than he should be doing for others in the world, and only a few days before his death he had arranged with me that should he be restored to health he would undertake to visit regularly and try to cheer some of the old people in the parish.'

But the best tribute to George Edward Meredith was paid by his daughter in her first published novel, *The Golden Arrow*. He is old John Arden, who keeps the lamp shining.

III

Spring breathed over the cradle of the child who was to become famous as Mary Webb. In the garden of her home at Leighton the daffodils were blowing, and the windy sunlight flashed across the lawn and on the windows to which her eyes turned in infant wonder. Beyond those windows, away to the north-east, the Wrekin towered in its solitude, dark with trees to the sharp summit, and brown and green along its lower slopes with ploughed fields and pastures.

A curiously contradictory hill, the Wrekin. At certain angles, seen from afar, it appears to be an unimposing hummock, at others it is as though an impressive mound had been heaped up by the labour of men for the especial purpose of catching the sunlight. Actually the Wrekin is a hill of grandeur and dignity; always it was to remain a living presence to Gladys Mary Meredith. Only when she lived in London was she unable to turn her eyes across the Shropshire distances and behold it in actuality – although she must surely have seen it clearer then, poignantly clearer than ever.

One of her brothers remembers how in girl-hood she would go out early in the morning and sit in the grass and watch the wild flowers open. She would watch them at evening too, seeing them close. He remembers also how she 'lay for hours and hours, just gazing at the wheatfield as the wind ran across it.' As one who is born in a house surrounded by storm-rocked trees will for ever be quick to hear their wild music even in treeless places, so enduring was the influence of Leighton on Gladys Mary Meredith. Leighton, from which the family moved when she was a year old, is ten miles out of Shrewsbury. The modern traveller approaches it most conveniently from Cressage. The scene is so little changed that if, leaving the single line of railway behind him, he pauses in his walk along the high road out of the village and stands on the bank above the river glittering in the sun at the time of the year when Mary Webb was born, he will know what peace filled that lush-leafed countryside half a century ago, when she as a child breathed its crystal air.

A peewit calls across the fleecy blue morning. There is hardly another sound, only an engine in the little railway station, half a mile away at

Cressage, fussily shunting trucks up and down and whistling, the noise fading into exaggerated echoes. But the world of movement is all beyond the horizon, a wooded horizon whereever the eye may range, for nothing gives a hint of life until, maybe, the clop-clop of a horse's hoofs is heard afar off, and soon a jogging trap appears round the corner of the winding road. When Mary Webb was a girl she always watched out with eager eyes for gipsies, and here, sure enough, a generation later, they come again. A brown-faced woman, with a coloured scarf round her head, is holding the reins, and a brown-faced boy sits beside her. Behind are two girls, leather-gaitered, in short workmanlike skirts, squeezing up against rolls of oilcloth that is hideously patterned and coloured. They stare without curiosity as they overtake and slowly pass the traveller. Soon they are lost between hedgerows along the road ahead, and clop-clop the old horse goes, jogging on to the village of Eaton Constantine or the neighbouring village of Leighton.

When Leighton emerges into view across the fields it is seen to be a cluster of grey roofs and red roofs, and one or two that are thatched and brown. Blossoming trees gleam everywhere, and dotted in the outlying neighbourhood are low-built farms, of beautifully mellowed brick that is almost buttercup-stained, against the green pastures. It was probably along the road to Cressage that in the spring following that of Gladys Mary Meredith's birth several heavily laden vans disturbed the ancient peace as they trundled away from Leighton. For in 1882 the Meredith family moved to Much Wenlock, an old Shropshire town on the Bridgnorth side of Wenlock Edge. It is likely that the Merediths went by way of Cressage to their new home at Much Wenlock. (The meaning of the 'Much' is plain when we note on the map that a near-by place is called Little Wenlock.) In any case the moving picture of the journey, so characteristic of the Shropshire whose 'burning ploughlands, faintly blue with wheat,' 'shadow-coloured hills,' 'purple lower slopes' where larches 'lie in lazy golden smoke, more faint, more still, than the pale wood-smoke of the cottage fire,' and 'slanting ways, in slanting sun,' must have been familiar at every step and turn, sooner or later, to the girl who eventually praised it all so proudly and gratefully in her prose and verse.

'Long, long ago I thought on all these things:
Long, long ago I loved them.'

. . . Probably, from her mother's arms as
she sat in the carriage that accompanied the
removal, the one-year-old Gladys Mary stared
out, round-eyed, at the crows' nests in the
trees high against the sky as they approached
the seven-arched, wooden toll-bridge, a hundred
years old, that, replaced since then by one
of stone, crossed the Severn near Cressage
station. Under the railway they would go, past
the ancient cross at Cressage, past the quaint
Eagles Inn, then up the steep hill until, looking
back, they were vouchsafed a farewell glimpse
of Leighton, three miles away, across the
valley.

Somewhere in the trees where the church
at Cressage rose grey-towered, a cuckoo would
call, perhaps, above the crunching wheels that
April day. Cottage gardens already radiant
with wallflower and primrose, and daffodil
edging the paths with yellow gold; the fields
of Cressage Park at the hill-crest, empty save
for storm-pools and a black crow in the middle
of the winter-washed green; the village of
Harley, with its round red tower, ivied walls

and trees; a smithy that rang with the busy anvil then, and rings with it still; signposts inscribed with delicious names – Hughley, Church Preen, Kenley, Wig-Wig! . . . barn-yard fowls and pigs, calves and sucklings. . . . All these lovely and pleasant features of an England which has not yet vanished must have left an abiding impression on that small child, too young to understand, but not too young to see them in her intervals of sleep.

Soon the ascent of Wenlock Edge began. Rugged and soft by turn is that Shropshire backbone: but nowhere so rugged that trees cannot grow. From near the height of the steep roadway, we may see, if we turn our heads, 'high the vanes of Shrewsbury gleam,' as A. E. Housman wrote in *A Shropshire Lad*; and beyond, far beyond, are the mountains of Wales (and the Wrekin, away to the right). But before that climb goes over Wenlock Edge itself the road straightens and runs through a deep ravine; as though man had suddenly grown tired of ascending, and re-solved to cleave the remainder of his way through the top. The last of the vast plain of western Salop slips from sight behind, and then, opening out ahead, another vale that spans a dozen miles to Worcestershire and Staffordshire. Immediately below Wenlock Edge, as cosily straggling as a fishing village on the cliff's edge, Much Wenlock nestles among the trees, blue-roofed, red-roofed, with the gaunt ruins of a priory in the midst of them, and a church eight centuries old.

Here came the Merediths of Leighton in 1882, father, mother and year-old daughter: here the family lived for fourteen years, and was increased by five children, Muriel, Kenneth, Douglas, Olive and Mervyn, all within seven years. And as we are seeking to trace Mary Webb's early development it may significantly be added that she had entered into her sixth year before any of her brothers or sisters was born.

IV

An elf-like child, brown-haired, blue-eyed: so active that she always seemed on tiptoe, eager for the first movement of a dance in the sunshine: so zestful and brisk, and yet so grave and thoughtful in her early years that there was something about her which suggested that in the years ahead, when she grew up, de Quincey's description of Wordsworth, 'the solemn and spiritual,' would be fitting for her also. Such was the small daughter of the Merediths, whom everybody called 'Glad,' and who is still remembered by old Shropshire folk as a solitary figure wandering along the laneways by Wenlock Edge, or trooping with her younger sisters and brothers down the winding avenue of trees, a quarter-mile long, that led into the Church Stretton high road from The Grange, the country house at which Mr. Meredith received and prepared more pupils for Sandhurst and the universities. Meadowland lay beyond that park-like garden, and cows, horses and poultry were kept there, tended by a coachman, a gardener and a cowman who always lived as well as worked in a smock.

In Mary Webb's writings we encounter that old cowman more than once. The short story entitled 'Owd Blossom' begins:

'Nobody knew his real name. Nobody wanted to know it. He had always been just "Owd Blossom"; always been considered simple. At the farms where he worked, his ungainly movements, his clumsy, unhandy ways could always

29

be relied upon to raise a laugh. He was very long, and thin, and knobby; his face went in where it should have gone out, and he wore a perpetual and almost fatuous smile.'

But it was not to mock at the old man's smile that she recalled it. Mary Webb sought to reveal what was beneath the smile, or what she believed to be beneath it, in 'the grave, wistful soul of the man,' where nobody had ever thought of looking. If anyone laughed at him for gathering flowers and showing as much pleasure in doing so as the other men of Wenlock showed in blowing froth from the rim of a pewter pot in the old inn-parlour or puffing at an old clay, he murmured, simply, 'I like a flower.'

And on Sunday afternoons, 'before he went to litter-down the stock for the night, he would lean over a gate, or lie on the hillside, and brood upon the plain. Nothing ever came of his broodings, at least there was never anything for anyone to see. He would shake back his flaxen hair, chew a stalk of bracken, and murmur "I like a sunset." That was all.'

But Owd Blossom was only one feature of the scene which presented itself to the observant

Mary Webb from her earliest days. It was not all sentimentally harmonious. There was discord also in her experience, and as a young girl she encountered it even on the threshold of her home, for she loathed the reason why her father kept beagles. In *Gone to Earth* we are given a hint of what she had witnessed or learnt by hearsay about hunting during those years at The Grange. *Gone to Earth* concludes with the symbolic double tragedy of Hazel Woodus and the fox; Hazel, the simple, lovely child of the forest, trapped and struggling to freedom, only to be trapped again, victim of the same cruelty that destroyed 'Foxy,' the 'smooth, white-bibbed personality,' towards whom she felt deeper affection and closer kinship than towards her far-from-wild husband.

'And as Hazel, dry-throated, whispered "Foxy!" and caught her up, the hounds came over the ridge like water. Riding after them, breaking from the wood on every side, came the hunt. Scarlet gashed the impenetrable shadows. Coming as they did from the deep gloom, fiery-faced and fiery-coated, with eyes frenzied by excitement, and open cavernous mouths, they were like devils emerging from hell on a foraging expedition.'

One of these devil-like beings was a huntswoman, 'her hair loose, and several of her pin-curls torn off by the branches,' determined to be in at the death. . . . The climax that comes swiftly is also the climax of the story.

'Hazel saw nothing, heard nothing. She was running with every nerve at full stretch, her whole soul in her feet. But she had lost her old fleetness, for Reddin's child had even now robbed her of some of her vitality. Foxy, in gathering panic, struggled and impeded her. She was only half-way to the quarry, and the house was twice as far.

' "I canna!" she gasped on a long terrible breath. She felt as if her heart was bursting.

'One picture burnt itself on her brain in blood and agony. One sound was in her ears — the shrieking of the damned. What she saw was Foxy, her smooth little friend, so dignified, so secure of kindness, held in the hand of the purple-faced huntsman above the pack that raved for her convulsive body. She knew how Foxy's eyes would look, and she nearly fainted at the knowledge. She saw the knife descend —

32

saw Foxy, who had been lovely and pleasant to her in life, cut in two and flung (a living creature, fine of nerve) to the pack, and torn to fragments. She heard her scream.

'Yes: Foxy would cry to her, as she had cried to the Mighty One dwelling in darkness. And she? What would she do? She knew that she could not go on living with that cry in her ears. She clutched the warm body closer.

'Though her thoughts had taken only an instant, the hounds were coming near. . . .'

The huntsmen and onlookers tried vainly to persuade her to separate herself from the fox. The little cleric, 'in his high-pitched nasal voice' called ' "Drop it! They'll pull you down!" while the large gold cross bumped up and down on his stomach.

'The death that Foxy must die, unless she could save her, dimmed all other sights and sounds. She gave one backward glance. The awful resistless flood of liver and white and black was very near. Behind it rose shouting devils.

'It was the death-pack.

'There was no hope. . . .' A moment later

the pack, with a ferocity of triumph, was flinging itself upon her.

'She was gone with Foxy into everlasting
silence. She would make no more honey from
the rosy flowers, nor dance like a leaf in the
wind.' And every man and woman 'crouched
and shuddered like beaten dogs,' and 'even the
hounds, raging on the quarry edge, cowered
and bristled' as the terrible cry once more
roused the shivering echoes:

' "Gone to earth! Gone to earth!" '

v

None can say what agonizing personal
memory had haunted Mary Webb since her
girlhood that she should take this opportunity
of pouring forth her hatred of hunting and its
inevitable stupidity as well as cruelty. It is well
to note that her emphasis is laid on the stupidity. For Gladys Meredith, we are assured by
those who knew her best, had no morbidity of
mind. Highly imaginative though she was, and
unattracted by the ordinary pursuits of the
children of her own age, holding aloof when the
more robust members of the family found
abundant scope for rollicking games suited to

34

their vigorous young natures; she was a normal child none the less, except that the trees, leaves, buds, flowers, fruit, wind and water, clouds, meadow and woodland, and all the ways and work and scenes of the countryside, gave her an acuter joy than other children knew. 'As a child,' she said later, 'I remember standing awe-stricken at the strange beauty of a well-known field in the magic of a June dawn.' And still lingering on remembered loveliness, she wrote:

'Oh, how I could mind it, on those still Sunday mornings when I went to the well, and would set down the buckets for a little while, and go out into the cornfields that lay beneath the vasty blue peace of the sky like creatures satisfied and at rest! There would be small birds about, making low contented cries and soft songs. There would be a rustling breeze, and rooks far up the sky, and a second bloom of pale gold flowers on the honeysuckle against the blue. There would be warmship that lapped you round, and the queenly gift of the scent of corn. What other scent is like it? There is so much in it beyond other sweets. There is summer in it and frosts. There is water in it, and the heart of the flint which the corn has taken up into its hollow stalks. There is bread in it, and life for man and beast.'

She did not fail to join the other children during their playtime – on bonfire night, for instance, when the fifth of November was celebrated by a great conflagration in the meadow opposite the house, and it was the enterprising Gladys who introduced the 'turnip lanterns' which made the occasion at The Grange famous with the juvenile population of the countryside. Nor did she fail to discern the quaintness of Much Wenlock itself, which she afterwards called 'a very Rip Van Winkle of a borough' that had fallen asleep somewhere in the Middle Ages, 'and if you should wonder at the fashion of its garments, you must remember that it had not, since the day it fell asleep, changed its coat, its hosen or its hat.' She found plenty to appeal to her developing sense of humour, notably in the spectacle of the old beadle in Much Wenlock church, who would rap unruly lads on their round heads with his staff, 'till you would think a woodpecker had come to church.'

She amply compensated the old man for laughing at him, though, when she was sent once a week to read the Bible to him. 'That was a great adventure!' she wrote in the story called 'Many Mansions.'

'There was the walk of a mile down the country road, beside which ran a thread of a brook, except in the summer. In the hedge-banks grew a few sweet violets, and there you might find the largest, most brightly coloured snail shells I have ever seen. But one must not linger too long, for down there, in the pool of hyacinth made by the valley shadows and the gentle smoke of hearth fires, John Lloyd waited to hear about the Many Mansions.

'On then, down the broad road between the sloping fields of miraculous green, past the roaring smithy. . . . Up three hollow steps into the dusky room, silent as one of the porches of eternity, and there was John in his Windsor chair, his black and yellow wand beside him, his great black Bible, so heavy that it made my arms ache, ready on the deal table.

' "Come thy ways in, my dear," he would say. "And God be with ye. A grand morning, seemingly."

' "Grand, John. And here's a snail shell in case you'd like a game of conker."

' "Nay, my dear, I be past conker. You keep it."

' "Then I'll put it in my faery house."

' "Ah. You do."

' "What shall I read, John?"

'He made a great show of considering, saying, "Well, there's a good few nice pieces. There's 'The greatest of these.' Then there's 'The pitcher be broken at the fountain,' and 'I will give you rest.' Then he would pause, and in a moment say, as if it were a totally new idea:

' "How about the Many Mansions piece, my dear?"

'I had no need to look for it; the book always fell open just there.'

VI

It was at The Grange, Much Wenlock, that one who became Gladys Mary Meredith's life-long friend, and was with her when she died, Miss E. M. Lory, joined the family. When Miss Lory first met Gladys she had passed her tenth year, and

'I saw at once,' Miss Lory recalls, 'that she had a very sweet nature, and, next to the father whom she adored, she was the most unselfish of

a fine-natured household. She was devoted to
her younger brothers and sisters, and her care
of them gave her an old-fashioned, motherly
way as a girl. I helped her with her studies for
the next four years. She was always ready to
learn. She would sit by the hour while I read
Shakespeare to her, and she grew to love the
plays more than anything in literature. Perhaps her writing was fostered by this regard for
Shakespeare, although she had written little
things from the age of six because her father
wrote and she strove to emulate him in most
things – I have some small paintings in an
album signed Gladys Meredith, and they are explained by the fact that he sketched and painted
too. It was at six that she began a poem with:

    ' "The rivers ran from rock to rock
      In the old, old days above." '

When she was twelve or thirteen, Miss Lory
remembers, she ransacked her mother's chests
and wardrobes without permission and borrowed a lot of beautiful and elaborate silks in
which to dress her younger brothers and sisters
so that they would represent flowers or fairies.
One became a poppy, one a forget-me-not, one
a daffodil, and another a favourite fairy char-

acter; then she composed suitable verses to be pinned upon the small players and taught them to enter the room turn by turn and recite. She was always planning and arranging, sometimes charades, sometimes plays. She dressed them on another occasion as the characters in *Alice in Wonderland*, one as the Walrus, another as the Carpenter, and so on. 'They looked exactly like Tenniel's drawings.' At Christmas she built up a large Christmas tree, and thought how nice it would be to invite the cottage children to a party. She made a present for each child, and went round to their homes herself to make sure how many were coming. She thought it very funny, one Christmas, when she knocked at a cottage door and asked the woman who opened it: 'How many children have you, please?' 'I'm an unmarried spinster,' the woman answered tartly, shutting the door in her face.

As a girl of thirteen or fourteen Gladys Mary went to Southport, Lancashire, to be a pupil at Mrs. Walmsley's finishing school. She was an earnest worker, especially at languages, and she had learned her French verbs so well that her teacher at Southport was frankly incredulous. 'Do you know,' said the indignant girl when she returned home, 'they thought I cheated!'

This hatred of injustice, which in her case was the natural corollary of a sense of pity, afterwards became one of Mary Webb's main characteristics. A valuable portrait, taken about this time, emphasizes its vital presence in her as a girl, no less than it emphasizes the other qualities of which she had given ample manifestation during her Wenlock days – strength and determination, acute sensitiveness, independence, candour and humour. . . .

Such was the girl who at the age of sixteen bade farewell to The Grange with the rest of the household and removed to Stanton-on-Hine Heath, which lies about five or six miles north of Shrewsbury town. By train they would go this time, changing at Buildwas Junction, nearby the noble remains of Buildwas Abbey, that was once the home of the Cistercian monks. Also near Buildwas stands a high ruined wall that is a decayed relic of temporal power built by the slaves of imperial Rome. 'Virocon, Virocon,' Mary Webb sang later –

'Still the ancient name rings on
And brings, in the untrampled wheat,
The tumult of a thousand feet.'

41

When she was a girl the excavations at that place had been proceeding for thirty years. So far they had revealed the centre of an important Roman city, Viroconium or Virconin. Doubtless her father explained to her that the city had been built soon after the defeat of the great Caractacus, and in its prosperity must have been larger than Pompeii. He would probably describe (watching for the deepening wonder in her face) the huge building whose ruined wall had been unearthed, that once enclosed the courts of law, the money mart, and the assembly hall where the people used to gather on momentous occasions. And even as he spoke she saw the Roman market, and the covered way on which patrician citizens met and passed the time of day, and as he described how the old Watling Street had been traced there she heard again 'the tumult of a thousand feet.'

She was a poet when, years afterwards, she returned to that ghostly city and in 'Viroconium' gave substance to her emotional musings.

'Where trumpets rang and men marched by
None passes but the dragon-fly.

Athwart the grassy town, forlorn,
The lone dor-beetle blows his horn.

*   *   *

'And still the breaking seas of grain
Flow havenless across the plain:
The years wash on, their spindrift leaps
Where the old city, dreaming, sleeps.

*   *   *

'The skulls of men who, right or wrong,
Still wore the splendour of the strong,
Are shepherds' lanterns now, and shield
Their candles in the lambing field.

'But when, through evening's open door,
Two lovers tread the broken floor,
And the wild apple petals fall
Round passion's scarlet festival;

'. . . There haunts within them secretly
One that lives while empires die,
A shrineless god whose songs abide
Forever in the countryside.'

Mary Webb's sense of nearness to those
ancient men who 'still wore the splendour of the
strong' must have been quickened as she and
her brothers and sisters gazed out upon the
drifting scene from the railway train that carried

43

them to their new home at Stanton-on-Hine Heath, for her mother suddenly pointed to a faint cluster of trees and roofs under the far Wrekin and said: 'Look, Glad, that is Leighton, you were born over there.' . . . And so they returned to the fringe of her first home-place, but only for as long as the train halted in the little station at Cressage. Soon it was bumping along the single track again, the white engine-smoke mirrored in the Severn as the river wound through the near-by fields, always within sight of the young traveller who was journeying into the mysterious unknown of a new home in a new part of the country. Nevertheless it was Shropshire still, nor did she cross the boundary into an alien world until she had become a grown woman, endowed with a purpose beyond that of ordinary womanhood. It was at Stanton-on-Hine Heath that she became seriously ill, and from a period of consequent inactivity she emerged as the creative artist whose gift, later on, was hailed and exalted by a Prime Minister of England.

CHAPTER TWO

Woman-Grown – the 'Soldier of Suffering'

I

IT was near the end of their sojourn at Stanton-on-Hine Heath that Gladys Mary Meredith became an invalid. Her age was sixteen when they went from Much Wenlock to that blossom-fragrant, bird-haunted house, then known as The Woodlands, afterwards re-named Harcourt Manor, close to Hawkstone Park and, as one of the family has described, 'five miles from anywhere.' The task allotted to her by her mother when she left the finishing-school at Southport was the difficult one of supervising the studies of her younger brothers and sisters. The exertion of this, aggravated through a strain caused by riding a bicycle, affected her so heavily that she collapsed soon after her twentieth birthday. The illness that ensued was diagnosed as Graves's Disease, and it was this that, recurring more than twenty years later, was one of the causes of her premature death.

Doubtless her native sense of responsibility became abnormal when the work of teaching

45

the younger members of her own family was entrusted to her — unfortunately entrusted to her, for the studious earnestness that she brought to it is not equipment enough for such a vocation, especially if its difficulties are increased by the pupils' lack of the discipline that would be imposed upon them by a stranger. Gladys Mary Meredith had always been uncommonly conscientious. Her conscientiousness made her scrupulously and fearlessly fair. This was shown vividly on an occasion before she was in her 'teens, when Mrs. Meredith gave the younger children their first lessons in reading, and found them annoyingly unreceptive.

To her accusation that they were only pretending not to know they responded with tears. Whereupon their eldest sister stoutly defended them with the argument that as their mother was not *inside* of them, how could she possibly know what they knew?

This attitude was expressed later on with a certain juvenile ruthlessness — the ruthlessness which she showed towards one of her sisters who complained of being 'not very well' and yet, although she was permitted to go and lie down instead of doing lessons, was soon heard romping about the room overhead. Gladys considered that this was 'not fair.' Her sister had escaped lessons by a deception; and, moreover, perceived that the deception was profitable, for she practised it again next day. Their governess had soothed Gladys with: 'Wait until she does it again,' and this time the young deceiver was dosed with quinine, at which Gladys was satisfied.

Lest this anecdote should suggest that there was a streak of priggishness in the girl, it must be added that those who remember her never thought of her as in any way priggish. She may not have been very fond of the ball games in which other children take delight, but she lived an open-air girlhood, all the same. She preferred to eat her meals on the grass out of doors rather than at the dining-table. The game in which she best liked to join was the old-fashioned one of 'hare and hounds.' She loved to wander about the countryside, especially in the company of her father, who helped her in the eager search for knowledge of trees, birds and flowers. She formed quaint friendships among the villagers, and the loving portraits she made of them are to be found in her books. Later in life as she moved through the lanes and fields, she would say excitedly to her companions: 'See, there's old So-and-So in my story.' And neither 'old So-and-So' nor the other originals showed anything but pride of his or her literary immortality.

She is still spoken of in the cottages as a young woman of dark brown, straight hair, and greyish-brown eyes whose expression changed with her mood. There is an amusing memory of the mood that prevailed most often. When she learnt that a litter of kittens would have to be destroyed she resolved that they should have a nice last meal, and gave them sardines.

She retained her childishness in many pretty ways. She delighted in a little musical box which, shaped like a grand piano, concealed a work-box, vanity-bag and mirror. The grand piano opened, and your eyes gazed at their own reflection as you listened to the tinkling old-time music!

II

When, in her twenty-first year, Mary Webb's health broke down, the illness was complicated by sundry bodily ailments, and before she was fully recovered the family had again changed their home, moving to Meole Brace, a village two miles south of Shrewsbury. For a long time she lay in bed or on the couch that was carried, when the day allowed, to the open window or down to the lawn at Stanton-on-Hine Heath or at 'Maesbrook,' the name of the new home; and then it was that Fate, in its notoriously ironical fashion, offered the invalid her opportunity. During her enforced leisure she began to write essays and poems, tentatively yet seriously, and one or two of them have been preserved. Some verses which she copied into an album for Miss Lory, her friend, are to be valued as the first known example of her work:

'Nature has opened her gates again!
    Her gates of gold and green;
Has opened them widely to welcome me
    Back to her glorious liberty,
To her wholesome grass and sun and rain
    Through the gates of gold and green.

'The Infinite sky bends close to me
    With a great protecting calm.
And waves upon waves of its peace profound
    Steal on my spirit, and circle me round
With the stillness of Eternity
    And a great protecting calm.'

Apart from the bibliographical justification this slight piece is entitled to a place in the story of Mary Webb's development because it illustrates an intensely grateful and reverent nature. So is another early example, which, entitled 'Elsewhere,' and dedicated 'To the Soldiers of Suffering,' is a natural outcome of her own years in the service of 'Captain Pain.'

'There's a great army that never sleeps,
    The army of suffering folk,
Still, through the centuries, watch it keeps
    Though it groans beneath the yoke.
You find its soldiers the whole world round
    Tormented in body or mind,
Shut out alike from the life of the world
    And the work and the joys of their kind.

'But a work of its own this army has!
    Each soldier must learn to bear
With patience whatever his Captain, Pain,
    Allots for his special share,
And the army's work is to stand and wait
    Outside the gates of pleasure
Inactive, away from the work of men
    In a forced, unwilling leisure.

'The raw recruits rebel at first
    In impotent misery,
Until they learn that discipline
    Will make them brave and free.
Some are discharged from the army's ranks,
    Having served well awhile,
But others stay on till the end of life,
    Meeting what comes with a smile.

'Up and down through the thronging ranks
    Passes the messenger Death,
And to the best-trained veterans,
    "Follow elsewhere," he saith,
Then they follow him out with shining eyes,
    For a whisper has gone round
That a great reward is given Elsewhere,
    To those who are faithful found.

' "Never again," so the whisper runs,
    "Shall we have to stand and wait:
We shall be sent on the King's own work,
    We shall pass through joy's bright gate,
And if here and elsewhere we do our best
    Maybe, so the rumours run,
We shall stand some day by the King's own
        Throne,
    And the King will say: Well done!" '

These verses indicate Mary Webb's early attitude of devotion, which had been given formality at her confirmation by the Bishop of Hereford when she was fourteen. One of her gifts to Miss Lory was a slim paper-bound volume entitled *The Sermon in the Hospital*, by Harriet Eleanor Hamilton. Here again is evidence at once of her piety and a preoccupation with her own physical handicap: —

'Now I heard
Fra Ugo Bassi preach. For though in Rome
He held no public ministry this year,
On Sundays in the hospital he took
His turn in preaching, at the service held
Where five long chambers, lined with suffering
     folk,
Converged, and in the midst an altar stood,
By which on feast-days stood the priest, and
     spoke,
And I remember how, one day in March,
When all the air was thrilling with the spring,
And even the sick people in their beds
Felt, though they could not see it, he stood
     there;
Looking down all the lines of weary life,
Still for a little under the sweet voice,

The
Sermon by the
Hospital

WHEN MARY WEBB WAS A GIRL: A BOOK-COVER
DESIGNED BY HER IN COLOURED WOOL

And spoke this sermon to them, tenderly
As it was written down by one who heard. . . .'

Doubtless she found consolation in such cheerful precepts of resignation as: 'Whoso suffers most hath most to give,' and 'What we win and hold is through some strife,' and 'Nay, we were fashioned not for perfect peace in this world, however in the next,' and 'Let me go back and suffer yet awhile more patiently': for

'When God formed in the hollow of His hand
This ball of Earth among the other worlds
And set it in His shining firmament,
Between the greater and the lesser lights,
He chose it for the Star of Suffering.'

That she thought highly of the booklet containing these lines is shown in the fact of her enclosing the presentation copy to her friend with strong cardboard covers and binding them with brown canvas, on which she embroidered a sampler of pale silk with the title of the poem in golden thread and a decoration of green leaves and purple berries. Unless a book is especially well thought of it does not call forth such uncommon trouble as that.

III

But she had also read *A Shropshire Lad*, by Professor A. E. Housman, that had been issued several years later, and it is certain that a profounder influence on her outlook lay in such trenchant poetry of her own countryside as Housman's lines beginning:

'Loveliest of trees, the cherry now
Is hung with bloom along the bough,
And stands about the woodland ride
Wearing white for Eastertide,'

or:

'Oh see how thick the goldcup flowers
Are lying in field and lane
With dandelions to tell the hours
That never are told again,'

or:

'In summertime on Bredon
The bells they sound so clear;
Round both the shires they ring them
In steeples far and near,
A happy noise to hear.'

We have, moreover, plain evidence in her poem 'Viroconium,' written in maturity, that Housman's influence on her was deep enough to last, however fleeting the effect of the hospital sermon. She pictured in 'Viroconium,' as we have seen, a place of untrampled wheat, where shepherds now pass to the lambing and lovers tread, and 'the wild-apple petals fall round passion's scarlet festival,' but where trumpets once rang and men marched by with the tumult of a thousand feet, so that to-day on capital and corridor lies the pathos of the supreme conqueror, Time. In *A Shropshire Lad*, Professor Housman described how 'on Wenlock Edge the wood's in trouble, his forest fleece the Wrekin heaves':

'The gale, it plies the saplings double,
And thick on Severn snow the leaves.
'Twould blow like this through holt and
    hanger
When Uricon the city stood. . . .
To-day the Roman and his trouble
Are ashes under Uricon.'

Housman and Shakespeare: these were the first among the abiding influences in the growth of Mary Webb the poet. Her mentality, moreover, was not long in outgrowing the influence of devout books and such devotional exercises as that of attending her father's Bible-reading with the rest of the family each morning and evening. For she read polemical authors, notably Darwin and Haeckel, and the consequences were vital. One of her brothers attended her progress through *The Origin of Species* and *The Riddle of the Universe*.

'I was a very serious-minded youth,' he writes, 'and being seven years younger I followed her eagerly. In all my studies I was greatly helped by her. We had long discussions about everything under the sun, and when, later, I went out into the world, we continued our discussions by correspondence. Another book I especially recall in her reading is *The Birth of Worlds and Systems*, because we had lots of arguments about it. The result of all this proved to be a pagan one. Her God was Nature.'

IV

Books, however, only clarified the emotions and sensations to which she became acutely receptive when, still in her convalescent period, she and the household arrived at Meole Brace. 'Maesbrook' was an old sixteenth-century house, and here Gladys Mary Meredith remained until her marriage at the age of thirty. To the inevitable experience of love and death was added in her case the exceptional one of becoming a creative artist. She could often be seen at her window, looking thoughtfully out across the garden and fields. Those early days of her lingering convalescence at Meole Brace were momentous. Her love of Nature, by this time pagan and whole-hearted, was intensified through the scene which began at her door, in a curving carriage-drive and a grassy slope that led to a shrubbery and a stream beyond the garden. Her gaze would sweep away past a copse of larches, past fields that climbed to the horizon, over which lay the road that afterwards led her dreaming step along the slow rise to Lyth Hill that ere long was luring her with pencil and writing-pad day after day in the early morning. Away to the left of the house ran a narrow laneway to the church that welcomed her in due time as a bride. The house at Meole Brace has been pulled down, and a new villa erected in its stead. The garden is different too, but the rippling brook at the end of it that runs quietly across the laneway still whispers the music that Mary Webb once heard and to which she half-listened as she pondered for long dream-rich mornings.

Neither has the music of other waters, the deep sound of a waterfall, been hushed. It is everywhere. Overhanging the waters of the brook are the same lovely old trees, whose roots can be seen twisted beneath the sluggish surface. Farther on is a deep stream with swifter waters, tree-bordered the whole way, dappled with white ducks, and if you turn your head as you watch them gliding lazily along you may see the chimneys of 'Maesbrook.' The pathway beyond the stream still beckons us through the fields, through delicious nooks and glens, green valleys, past the first cottage with its quaint announcement of trade and barter: 'Bees, Queens, Hives, and Appliances, Extracted and Combed Honey'. The artist in Mary Webb did not overlook this, for in *Gone to Earth* one of the exhibits at the village show is Abel Woodus's honey, announced on a large placard inscribed by himself in drunken capitals:

'ABEL WOODUS. BEE-MAN.
COFFINS. HONEY. WREATHS.

Open to engagements to play the Harp at Weddings, Wakes, and Club-days. . . .'

But to-day it is the stranger who follows the

track of that pathway, not the woman for whom it opened on to a visionary world, an 'other life' that, through her books, has become for many people as real as the world we know.

v

The 'other life' of the green earth, which was being revealed to Mary Webb ever since she stood awe-stricken as a child 'at the strange beauty of a well-known field in the magic of a June dawn,' has its imaginative interpretation in the twelve nature studies that comprised the first complete work of her literary career, entitled *The Spring of Joy*. The publication of this work took place in 1917, when she was thirty-six, a year after the appearance of her first novel, but written earlier. We must assume that *The Spring of Joy* was the author's first selection among a large number of essays written since she made her tentative beginnings in authorship at Stanton-on-Hine Heath.

The immediate characteristic which we note in them is the sensitiveness that made her Nature-love so intimate. This sensitiveness had expressed itself in her everyday life when her parents decided that a high hedge of hawthorn

59

on the border of one of the fields at Meole Brace, having become an obstruction, would have to be cut down. 'I remember after all these years,' writes Miss Lory, 'how distressed she was. She implored her father, she pleaded with her brothers to help her to save the hedge. It would break her heart, she said, if the old hawthorn were cut down. . . .'

The Spring of Joy is the work of one who is aspiring rather than achieving, one who has taken upon herself the task of maintaining an English tradition of Nature essay-writing that was by her time well established. It needs little comparative study to perceive that her models were Richard Jefferies and 'Fiona Macleod.' 'The power of this life' – Mary Webb is speaking of 'the passion that fills all nature,' the unknown quantity, the guarded secret 'that dwells in the comet, in the heart of a bird, and the flying dust of pollen':

'The power of this life,' she writes, 'if men will open their hearts to it, will heal them, will create them new, physically and spiritually. Here is the gospel of earth, ringing with hope, like May mornings with bird-song, fresh and healthy as fields of young grain. But those who would be healed must absorb it not only into their bodies in daily food and warmth but into their minds, because its spiritual power is more intense. It is not reasonable to suppose that an essence so divine and mysterious as life can be confined to material things; therefore, if our bodies need to be in touch with it so do our minds. The joy of a spring day revives a man's spirit, reacting healthily on the bone and the blood, just as the wholesome juices of plants cleanse the body, reacting on the mind. Let us join in the abundant sacrament – for our bodies the crushed gold of harvest and ripe vine-clusters, for our souls the purple fruit of evening with its innumerable seeds of stars.'

Almost this passage might have been quoted from 'Fiona Macleod's' *Where the Forest Murmurs* or Richard Jefferies' *The Story of My Heart*. Actually it belongs to the opening essay of Mary Webb's *The Spring of Joy*. Thus her personal creed is to be identified, more or less closely, with that of the ecstatically emotional William Sharp ('Fiona Macleod') and with that of the ecstatically intellectual Jefferies. 'We live the life of plants, the life of animals, the life of men, and at last the life of spirits,'

61

wrote Sir Thomas Browne long ago, expressing, as Mary Webb reminds us, a whole philosophy in one sentence. The flowers and fruit, the trees with their leaf and bud; the hills and mountains and valleys, and the wild and tame creatures that range over them; the clouds and rivers, meadows, woods and forests – these have all a 'oneness,' 'it is this that sends one man to the wilds, another to dig a garden; that sings in a musician's brain; that inspires the pagan to build an altar and the child to make a cowslip-ball.' 'If a Sparrow comes before my Window,' wrote John Keats in a letter, 'I take part in its existence, and pick about the gravel.' Mr. W. H. Davies makes an all-round declaration of the same sense of unity in his poem 'The Elements.'

'No house of stone
　　Was built for me;
When the Sun shines –
　　I am a bee.

'No sooner comes
　　The Rain so warm,
I come to light –
　　I am a worm.

'When the Winds blow,
   I do not strip,
But set my sails —
   I am a ship.

'When Lightning comes,
   It plays with me
And I with it —
   I am a tree.

'When drowned men rise
   At Thunder's word,
Sings Nightingale —
   I am a bird.'

'The winds are our playfellows,' declared
Mary Webb, having experienced with all these
mystics what she called, in another passage,
'the sudden sense — keen and startling — of
oneness with all beauty, seen and unseen.' The
revelation invariably coloured her writings,
essay, verse, novel. *The Spring of Joy* is therefore to be accepted as a first proclamation of
faith, gradually built up as she lay on her sickbed and in the time of recovery that followed
her removal to Meole Brace. If for no other
reason than this the essays are important to the
student of her work. But they have a claim on
the reader in their own right. The stuff of

poetry is there – the passage already quoted, 'the purple fruit of evening with its innumerable seeds of stars,' is one of many whose impression is that of a flash of poetry. When Mr. Walter de la Mare contributed an introduction to the volume on its appearance in the Collected Works of Mary Webb, he wrote: 'Few observers háve taken the pains to describe an object so minute in terms so precise, yet the words are poetical in effect: they are charged with life and significance, and only a loving rapture in the thing itself could have found them for this purpose.'

The majority of the essays are variations on a single theme. They convey the moral of the philosophy of 'oneness.' It brings a depth of understanding and sympathy that fills the possessor with such tolerance, comfort, loving-kindness and love, that nature would brim over with beauty, joy and harmony, as it nearly does already, if all humanity could breathe the same deep breath of awareness as individual men and women do. As for the effect on these individual men and women, whoever has been blind and even hopeless heretofore will see that 'through His coming the thickets are quickened into leaf and touched with glory'. 'Out in this world the spirit that was so desolate, lost in the strange atmosphere of physical inferiority, may once more feel the zest that he thought was gone for ever. And this zest is health: sweeping into the mind and into the recesses of being beyond the conscious self, it overflows into the body.'

Here the mental effect of Mary Webb's long sickness is as manifest as it had been in her choice of *The Sermon in the Hospital* as a book for presentation to her friend. She had obviously experienced at one period a desolating sense of 'the strange atmosphere of physical inferiority,' and a wistful aspiration that has for its source a profound truth:

'This zest is health: sweeping into the mind and into those recesses of being beyond the conscious self, it overflows into the body. Very often this first rush of joy, this drinking of the freshets of the divine, brings back perfect health. Even in diseases that are at present called incurable, and that are purely physical, no one will deny the immense alleviation resulting from this new life.'

Not only alleviation, she believes as she pursues her logic more and more eagerly, but an attainment of the sublime state in which 'there shall be no more sorrow, no more pain, and the tears shall be wiped from every eye.' 'It is possible that, as the spiritual ties between man and nature grow stronger, all disease may vanish before the vitality that will stream into us so swiftly, so easily, because it will not be confined to one channel.'

Although Mary Webb recovered from her early illness, she was never to achieve the complete triumph of mind. We are told that the peculiar form of that illness affected her so much and so markedly that her extreme sensitiveness led her to write in *The Spring of Joy* about finding refuge in Nature because the wild creatures don't start away from you. A few brief years of work, bringing a success not to be belittled or complained about overmuch, and the malady returned. It is a poignant thought, in the light of what circumstances have revealed since, that when she was battling against recurrent ill-health during her five years in London, only a stone's throw from her Hampstead cottage another stricken woman-writer was undergoing a similar struggle. Unknown to each other, Mary Webb and Katherine Mansfield were drawing near to the close of their lives without being aware that they could have reached out and clasped hands. They may or may not have been aware of each other's existence, but Katherine Mansfield might almost have written parts of 'Vis Medicatrix Naturae', the opening essay in *The Spring of Joy*: and Mary Webb wrote sketches that are not very distant, temperamentally and in their expression, from several of the more tender stories of Katherine Mansfield.

VI

The spirit of tragedy, that was in Mary Webb's novels later on, is to be felt throughout her essays, although she entitled the manuscript brightly enough, and although this 'little book of healing,' which is the sub-title, brims over with what Mr. de la Mare calls 'a grave and sweet happiness, the happiness "of the minds of the simple-hearted who are the Magi of the world." ' The very implication that there is something to be healed is tragic. 'Salvation' may end tragedy, but it cannot absolve it. Mary Webb's great certainty is that if we accept the avenue that takes us back to Nature we shall know 'the lovely ways that lead from our doors into the heart of enchantment.' We shall

67

not simply have 'Joy, Laughter and Beauty' – how wistful it sounds in her utterance, this definition of her sacred trinity! – but 'we shall know the way to other things, not less precious; we shall know of long, green vistas, carpeted with speedwell, ascending to a place of comfort, and the blue butterfly will lead us into peace.'

Like all writers who employ symbolism and imagery, Mary Webb sometimes becomes vague, verbose, and occasionally inconsistent. Thus she refers to 'the heart of enchantment' on the same page as she speaks of peace, apparently hoping to invoke a single idea – or even an ideal – and unless the reader is inclined to adopt an attitude of unquestioning responsiveness, that ought not to be taken for granted by a writer, she fails. Nevertheless, the faultiness of her early essay-writing does not debar us from a reasonable understanding of her early mind – an understanding which is very necessary for an appreciative survey of her progress. Again and again in her novels we shall encounter the grave yearning that led her to write 'The Joy of Motion' (whose introductory text is George Herbert's 'My free soul may use her wing'), with its Jefferies-like personalities – 'All summer you watch a pair of swallows; you seem to be getting to know them, to be nearer their secret'; or 'Evening after evening in the summer, I have gone to see the white clover fall asleep in the meadows. Kneeling and looking very closely, as the dew begins to gather, one sees a slight change in the leaves; all round, the green is paler than by day – when the dark upper surfaces of the leaves are flat beneath the flowers – because the pale undersides are now visible.' There is, incidentally, an obvious 'Fiona Macleod'-like conclusion to the paragraph: 'Everywhere in the dusk the white clover leaves are sleeping in an attitude of worship; those who are early enough may see them wake and rise in the morning – multitudes moving in slow unfaltering unity.'

And as with the essay on 'The Joy of Flight' so with the pæan to the joy of music that comes next in the volume. It is in Nature, of course, that Mary Webb hears the vocal and orchestral music which 'laughs and sobs through the seasons with eternal variations,' and the bright-throated quiver of the thrush 'singing in April on the high yew-bough' expresses the sentiment which she tries so doggedly, and yet not without a bird's lightness, to express on many a later page:

'Now in every country place the birds translate their happiness into delicious song. "Live! Laugh!" cries the chiff-chaff all day long, careless of elaborations if he can give his message, effectually cutting the silence with his two small notes like silver shears. The tom-tit, with characteristic egoism, shouts "Me, me, me!" The yellow-hammer and the hedge-sparrow tell over their short recurring staves. The green linnet sits erect, though his body sways with music; the notes come slipping through the leaves like rain, and sometimes he throws back his head, and laughs. The cheery babble of starlings fills any pauses, and the lark – Mercury of Spring – goes on skyey messages.

'Then one morning you wake to a consciousness of something more; across the lighter singing strikes the bourdon note of the cuckoo, expressing the same thing as cuckoos were saying when Watling Street was made, of which we long to know the interpretation. The willow-wrens begin their ethereal whisperings; the black-cap comes. He is the meistersinger of gardens where the nightingale is absent; in a moment, as you stand by the willow where he is, he opens the doors of delight. His swift, winning phrases go lilting up and down in continuous sweetness for an hour at a time. Then suddenly there are swallows, clinging to the eaves and to branches over water, chattering with lovely monotony, singing long songs that pass and come again – low, serene, contemplative.

'So all day between dusk and dusk there is music. . . .'

We behold vividly, at that passage, the child Gladys Mary Meredith, who 'would stand awe-stricken at the strange beauty of a well-known field in the magic of a June dawn': stand with Traherne and William Blake and all the visionaries whose visions came to them among the fields and valleys. We behold also the brooding invalid whose womanhood began on a sickbed, and who whispered to herself over and over that 'laughter need not be lost to those that are cut off from their fellows.'

And we know surely, while the last words of 'The Joy of Music' still echo, that only among those birds and the other 'earth children,' far from what she condemned as 'the foetid haunts of the money-grubbers,' Mary Webb can ever have been truly herself – there, where the music of earth 'summons us poor wanderers in tones reassuring as a herdsman's call to his cattle on the mountains – simple and homely.'

71

CHAPTER THREE

*Essays and Poems – 'O Sing Me Far Away, that
I May Hear the Voice of Grass . . .'*

I

WE shall do well to regard Mary Webb's
essays as a first record of the imaginative
and intellectual development whose eventual
outcome was the authorship of *Precious Bane*.
She had looked beyond the religion of piety
with which she was surrounded in her young
womanhood, and to which she responded so
completely that at one time she carried out the
duties of parochial visitor in the parish of
Meole Brace. But she had the mind of a
Nature-worshipper, rather than one to which
orthodox religion makes a lasting appeal. She
sought evidence of the divine purpose that
would better satisfy her nature-worshipping
mind, and confident, almost dogmatic, though
she is in *The Spring of Joy*, it was later on, in
Precious Bane itself, that she described how her
search was rewarded. She avoided, of course (as
an artist must avoid), the literal explanation; she
employed Prue Sarn as her spokeswoman, as
for example, when Prue tells how she found in

the attic at her brother's farm a refuge from misery:

'So, it being very still there, with the fair shadows of the apple trees peopling the orchard outside, that was void, as were the near meadows – Gideon being in the far field making haycocks, which I also should have been doing – there came to me, I cannot tell whence, a most powerful sweetness that had never come to me before. It was not religious, like the goodness of a text heard at a preaching. It was beyond that. It was as if some creature made all of light had come on a sudden from a great way off, and nestled in my bosom. On all things there came a fair, lovely look, as if a different air stood over them. It is a look that seems ready to come sometimes on those gleamy mornings after rain, when they say, "So fair the day, the cuckoo is going to heaven."

'Only this was not of the day, but of summat beyond it. I cared not to ask what it was. For when the nut-hatch comes into her own tree, she dunna ask who planted it, nor what name it bears to men. For the tree is all to the nut-hatch, and this was all to me. Afterwards, when

I had mastered the reading of the book, I read:

"His banner over me was love,"

and it called to mind that evening. But if you should have said, "Whose banner?" I couldna have answered. And even now, when Parson says "It was the power of the Lord working in you," I'm not sure in my own mind. For there was naught in it of churches nor of folks, praying nor praising, sinning nor repenting. It had to do with such things as bird-song and daffadowndillies rustling, knocking their heads together in the wind. And it was as wilful in its coming and going as a breeze over the standing corn.

'It was a queer thing, too, that a woman who spent her days in sacking, cleaning sties and beast-housen, living hard, considering over fardens, should come of a sudden into such a marvel as this. For though it was so quiet, it was a great miracle, and it changed my life; for when I was lost for something to turn to, I'd run to the attic, and it was a core of sweetness in much bitter.'

Prue Sarn had but to creep in there, Gladys Mary Meredith had but to 'hear the bees making their murmur and smell the woody, o'er-sweet scent of kept apples, and hear the leaves rasping on the window-frame, and watch the twisted grey twigs on the sky,' and she would 'forget all else' than the life of 'rose and gold' that shone with 'the glory which comes from the other side of silence.' For the divine purpose, she believed, was truly revealed in natural beauty, in the stirring of the sap and the re-birth of spring. God was a living God, who offered strength to mankind through the earth. This truth was 'the core of sweetness in much bitter.' Her years of ill-health, in their confinement, had been a bitter thing: so was the knowledge that round about her there were hurt and suffering creatures: it was, indeed, her emotion at the threat to the high hawthorn hedge at Meole Brace which led eventually to a poem, 'To The World,' that has been preserved and included in the collected volume:

'You took the rare blue from my cloudy sky;
You shot the one bird in my silent wood;
You crushed my rose – one rose alone had I.
You have not known. You have not under-
    stood.

'I would have shown you pictures I have seen
Of unimagined mountains, plains and seas;
I would have made you songs of leafy green,
If you had left me some small ecstasies.

'Now let the one dear field be only field,
That was a garden for the mighty gods.
Take you its corn. I keep its better yield –
The glory that I found within its clods.'

II

Mary Webb's poems have an important place
in her spiritual development. Just as her prose
essays are an early record of her spiritual dis-
coveries, so her poems, in a similarly intense
way, and her novels, in a broader way (they
allowed more space for the unfolding of her
mind), may be said to emphasize the revelations
that came to her. Much of the verse included
in her collected volume is, of course, contemporary with the novels, even with the last of
them, for unlike many writers who have decided
that prose fiction is their principal medium, she
never neglected the form of expression that
she once regarded as urgent. Her technical
development in poetry was nevertheless swift.
Not only is there a marked contrast in craft

between the poems we have already quoted –
those written at the time of her illness, 'Nature
has opened her gates again!' 'Elsewhere,' dedicated to the 'Soldiers of Suffering,' and even
'To The World' – but almost in successive
pages of the collected volume made at the end
of her life, do we find a change from inexpert-
ness to maturity. It is seldom that her poems
have this maturity in the sense of completeness,
for only in a dozen of them did Mary Webb
reach the state that alone entitles a writer of
verse to be described as a poet. She rarely
emerged from the period of whose production
the reader is impelled to say: 'How like Alice
Meynell,' or 'How like John Drinkwater, or
Professor Housman.'

> 'Into the scented woods we'll go
> And see the blackthorn swim in snow.'

That is the beginning of a verse by Mary Webb.
Here is the beginning of one by Housman:

> 'About the woodlands I will go
> To see the cherry hung with snow.'

In the concluding lines of Mary Webb's 'Market Day' the poet suggests that:

'If all folk lived with labour sweet
Of their own busy hands and feet,
Such marketing, it seems to me,
Would make an end of poverty.'

In Mr. Drinkwater's 'Holiness,' written and published some years earlier, we read:

'If all the carts were painted gay
    And all the streets swept clean. . . .
If all the houses looked as though
    Some heart were in their stones. . . .
I think this gaiety would make
    A spiritual land,
I think that holiness would take
    This laughter by the hand,
    Till both should understand.'

Another poem – this time a sonnet – by Mary Webb confesses the weary striving for slumber that ends after 'eternities gone by' in love flowing around her 'with its calm and blessing,' and quiet sleep:

'I can but let it take me, and be still,
 And know that you, beloved, though far from
    me
All night are with me – comforting, caressing.'

In 'Renouncement,' also a sonnet, Alice Meynell confessed long since how:

'When night gives pause to the long watch I
        keep,
And all my bonds I needs must loose apart
Must doff my will as raiment laid away —
With the first dream that comes with the first
        sleep
I run, I run, I am gathered to thy heart.'

'Fairy Led,' by Mary Webb, opens with:

    'The fairy people flouted me,
      Mocked me, shouted me. . . .
    They chased me down the dreamy hill,
      and beat me with a wand.
    Within the wood they found me, put
      spells on me and bound me,
    And left me at the edge of day in John
      the Miller's pond.'

Mr. Alfred Noyes had already exploited the form in *Tales of the Mermaid Tavern*:

'As I came home by Sudbury, by little red-
        roofed Sudbury,
I waited for my bare-foot maid, among her
        satin kine.

79

I heard a peal of wedding bells, of treble, bass
    and tenor-bells:
"Ring well," I cried, "this bridal morn! You
    soon shall ring for mine!" '

In another of Mary Webb's poems she writes:

'Bring me an unguent made of scented roots;
Pomander of green herbs and scarlet fruits,
Verbena leaves, mallow and melilot,
And balmy rosemary. . . .'

This recalls Christina Rossetti's joyous request
in 'A Birthday':

'Raise me a dais of silk and down,
    Hang it with vair and purple dyes;
Carve it in doves and pomegranates
    And peacocks with a hundred eyes.'

All poets have been acutely impressionable
during their growth, especially when they have
encountered poems by others that embodied the
sentiments they feel, wistfully, that they in their
turn ought to put on paper and would do, given
the power. All poets have tried to recapture in
their admiring fashion the fancies of some
earlier poet's creation. Mary Webb was hardly
else than a sedulous admirer of others in such

pieces as 'Fairy Led,' 'How Short a While,'
'Market Day,' 'Green Rain,' and more notably
in 'Colomen,' her most ambitious piece of
writing in verse, that is haunted by Christina
Rossetti and Samuel Taylor Coleridge, and
always will be, for it was never finished.

'The doves that coo in Colomen
Are never heard by mortal men
But when a human creature passes
Underneath the churchyard grasses.
In deep voices, velvet-warm,
They tell of ancient perils, storm
Long hushed, and hopes withered and dead,
And joys a long while harvested. . . .

          *   *   *

'And still, at Colomen, they say,
When midsummer has stolen away
The last arch primrose, and swiftly fall
Hawthorn petals, wan as a pall,
And the grave blackbirds, that of late
Shouted the sun up, meditate,
You hear about the ruined cote
A mighty, muted sound of wings,
And faint, ghostly flutterings.
Then, if your death is near, you see
A lady standing like a tree

Bent down with blossom. Long ago
Her little joy, her long woe!

   *   *   *

'And from the house of Colomen,
Like water from a frozen strand,
Failed the voices of maids and men,
Shrivelled the heart, shrivelled the hand,
Till there within the arching wood
No face was left but the painted face,
No sound was left of the human race,
But only the sound of doves that cooed
Sadly, intermittently –
Wheeling doves that none can see
But dying men who wander here
And see a picture, glassy-clear,
Where the milky hawthorn-blossom falls
And from the elm a blackbird calls:
Then softly from the ruined cote
A pigeon coos – and faint, remote,
A hundred pigeons answer low,
Voicing the lady's ancient woe;
And then they see her, very fair
And fragile in the scented air;
On arms and shoulders doves alight,
Multiple-tinted, like a bright
Tapestry that time has faded.
Softly purple, lilac-shaded,

The lady standeth, like a tree
Bent down with blossom. . . .'

Technically, however, some of these poems written at highly impressionable moments represent Mary Webb at her best. They are free from such faults and infelicities as those which mark a piece called 'Starlings':

> 'They mimic in their glee
> With impudent jocosity
> The terrible ululation of the owls
> That prey
> On just such folk as they,'

or these, from another poem:

> 'In April, in April
> My heart is set' —

lines which are not strong enough as an opening, nor are they at all strengthened by those which follow immediately after:

> 'Where the pansy and the violet
> And the daffodil,
> And close-folded lilies grow
> In borders dark with melted snow.'

Often her rhymes are hackneyed, and there are lines which suffer from weak endings:

'Soft and bright,
Upon a water-kissing bough she lit
And washed and preened her silver breast,
    though it
Was dazzling fair before.'

She has delicacy of ear, and yet in 'Dust' she speaks of 'their *static* beauty only fit for tears,' thus marring the impression of one of her most successful pieces. Sir Sidney Colvin illustrates in his *Life of John Keats* what the unerring ear can do with a word or phrase that is not wholly satisfactory.

'One evening in the twilight, the two students sitting together, Stephens at his medical studies, Keats at his dreaming, Keats breaks out to Stephens that he has composed a new line:

"A thing of beauty is a constant joy."

"What think you of that, Stephens?" "It has the true ring, but it is wanting in some way." . . . An interval of silence, and again the poet:

"A thing of beauty is a joy for ever."

"What think you of that, Stephens?" "That it will live for ever." '

But the time came when her understanding of word-values ripened, although it was to give distinction to her novels rather than her poetry, which was spasmodic in her later period. Nevertheless she wrote a little group of poems which represent a definite achievement. And as we read them – these 'moments of thought captured,' as they have been happily called – we feel the dismay of broken music and wish she might have lived to pursue steadily again the art of which, in her fashion, she had undoubtedly taken the measure. We have a certain consolation in the rich ideal of peace those few poems convey to us. We come away from them somewhat as Enoch Gale in *The House in Dormer Forest* came away from the Birds' Orchard after 'waiting for what would come out of the unfathomable' – 'he turned to go down hill again in the dim morning with light in his face.'

The collection of eighty-three poems which are all that have been published sounds this dominant note of peace as the ideal at the very beginning, when, in 'Green Rain,' the poet describes the scented woods as so full of serene whisperings that almost it is 'as if a storm of rain had stood enchanted, . . . and, hearing fairy voices call, hung poised, forgetting how to fall.' The same suggestion of dreaming eagerness is in the very last lines of the book, for her unfinished poem 'Colomen' breaks off with the phrase 'A tree bent down with blossom.' These two poems, if we allow for influences, are to be included among her most successful. Others are 'The Happy Life' and 'Market Day,' with their curiously similar first lines:

'No silks have I, no furs nor feathers,
 But one old gown that knows all weathers' –
and

  'Who'll walk the fields with us to town,
   In an old coat and a faded gown?'

Never again was the writer Mary Webb to be as care-free and unconventional as in these wholehearted hymns that praise the life of 'rough hands and a tanned face,' a life that counts worldly riches as nothing, and as everything the riches of soft crinkled leaves, 'the cries of birds across the lawns in dark and teeming April dawns,' the sound of wings,

  'And the gay scent of the wood I burn
   And the slap of butter in the busy churn.'

In the lyric 'The Happy Life' there is only this single, utterly simple thought: but the poet thinks rather more in detail at the conclusion of 'Market Day.' After a similar enunciation of earth's allurements, which now are those of wild life, the blackbird, small caterpillars, startled lapwings, nesting dippers, and rabbits, she comes to market.

> 'Our shoes are golden as we pass
> With pollen from the pansied grass.'

Dinner follows:

> 'Beneath an elder — set anew
> With large clear plates to catch the dew —
> On fine white cheese and bread we dine:
> The clear brook-water tastes like wine.'

For details of the marketing itself — and how well she knew them in her own experience will be revealed later — we have to turn to another poem 'The Elf.' The market town, of course, is her own fair town of Shrewsbury — 'the world over you'll hardly find a fairer.'

> 'Early there come travelling
> On market day
> Old men and young men
> From far away,

87

'With red fruits of the orchard
And dark fruits of the hill,
Dew-fresh garden stuff,
And mushrooms chill,
Honey from the brown skep,
Brown eggs, and posies
Of gilly flowers and Lent lilies
And blush roses.'

Her simple pleasure in the mere tabulation of
these homely things of the English countryside
is as evident as Rupert Brooke's in 'The Great
Lover,' where he makes a catalogue of 'dear
names' – white plates and cups, feathery dust,
wet roofs beneath the lamplight, a crust of
bread, blue wood-smoke, rainbows, raindrops,
flowers, 'cool kindly sheets,' blankets, 'grainy
wood,' shining hair, clouds, hot water, furs to
touch, old clothes:

'Sweet water's dimpling laugh from tap or
    spring;
Firm sands: the little dulling edge of foam
That browns and dwindles as the wave goes
    home:
Sleep; and high places: footprints in the dew;
And oaks; and brown horse-chestnuts, glossy
    new,

And new peeled sticks; and shining pools on
    grass. . . .'

Mary Webb would have said with Rupert
Brooke that 'all these have been my loves'; and
turning to them, she could have echoed him in
the plea that after later lovers of such things
have praised them with 'All these were lovely'
they may remember him and add 'He loved.'
Seldom does she travel out of sight of homeliness in her poetry. In an occasional piece,
such as 'An Old Woman,' she attempts a
still-life picture, including a portrait, after the
eighteenth-century manner:

'They bring her flowers — red roses heavily
    sweet,
White pinks and Mary lilies and a haze
Of fresh green ferns: around her head and
    feet
They heap more flowers than she in all her
    days
Possessed.'

These are the opening lines of 'An Old
Woman,' but they only prepare the way for the
enunciation of a homily on what was, with her,
a favourite plaint — that we are over-fond of

bestowing gifts on the dead in whose lifetime it has never occurred to us to make such an offering. 'An Old Woman' was written, we are told, 'because it went against Mary Webb's grain to see flowers put on the graves in Meole Brace churchyard and never taken to the Meole Brace cottages.' Not only flowers were mistakenly given:

'Now in a new and ample gown she lies –
White as a daisy-bud, as soft and warm
As those she often saw with longing eyes . . .
This would have pleased her once. She does not care
At all to-night.'

There is no place for moralizing in a poet's pen-portrait, any more than there is in the portrait done with a painter's brush. That is why Mary Webb's venture into this kind of verse, after beginning with promise, concludes without making its intended impression, pathetic and tender though that conclusion is:

'They give her tears – affection's frailest flowers–
And fold her close in praise and tenderness:
She does not heed. Yet in those empty hours
If there had come, to cheer her loneliness,

But one red rose in youth's rose-loving day,
A smile, a tear,
It had been good. But now she goes her way
And does not hear.'

The poet is nearer success with her portrait of the one-time milkmaid who is now an old workhouse woman, because in this poem she eschews the laborious attempt to emphasize one of humanity's little failings. 'Going for the Milk' is a neat series of glimpses – of the child toddling on her errand; of the girl –

'Going for the milk
With laughing, teasing lads, at seventeen,
With rosy cheeks and breast as soft as silk –
Eh! what a mort of years between!' –

then of the young wife with her first baby sleeping on her arm during the errand, and lastly, of the woman fifty years later, dim-eyed, chilled in the cold workhouse ward, reflecting that –

'Never no more I'll go the flowery way,
Fetching the milk. I drink the pauper's skim,
And mind me of those summer days, and Jim
Telling me as my breast was soft as silk –
And that first day I missed to fetch the milk.'

In so few lines does Mary Webb gain her effect that her failure to persist with this especial kind of poetry is to be regretted. Her pastoral experience gave her many subjects for character portrayal, she had a true and generous attitude to them, and her exploitation of them in prose-fiction could not have debarred her from a corresponding exploitation in verse – it did not debar Thomas Hardy in the case of *Tess of the D'Urbervilles*. Nor was she one of the artists who lose interest in a subject when they have worked on it once only, for her novels are peopled with many characters of a common origin – as, for example, the philanderers, Ralph Elmer, of *Seven for a Secret*, and Peter, of *The House in Dormer Forest*, or the false lovers, Gillian and Ruby, in the same two novels respectively, and Lily of *The Golden Arrow*.

In the main, however, she was content to be a reflective poet, and, even so, she failed to retain the mood of 'The Happy Life' and 'Market Day.' Soon we find her dwelling on the idea of parting – not simply in the sense of 'Good-bye to Morning' –

'I will say goodbye to morning, with her eyes
Of gold, her shell-pale robe and crocus-crown.
    . . . the wind of evening grieves
In the changing wood' –

but in the sense of complete farewell to all that she has loved. 'How softly painted flushes Death above me!' she exclaims in 'Winter Sunrise,' and in 'Hunger' she writes: 'I would from life's severe detention arise and go.' There is a poem with the actual title 'Farewell,' and another is called 'Farewell to Beauty.' It must be allowed, moreover, that 'Farewell to Beauty,' and 'The Difference,' a shorter meditation on the theme, are among her successes.

In 'The Difference' we see her walking 'among the daisies, as of old,' but walking alone, for 'he comes never more, by lane or fold.' A year ago they had been together and seen the same flowers – 'Last May! Last May! A century ago.' In the warm speedwell-field, dark with dew, there is a rosy tree from which he plucked an apple-bough; but –

'Not all the blossom on the branches left
 Can fill the place of that sweet bough bereft.'

So skilfully has the impression been built up that the poignancy of the final line 'Last May! Last May! Eternities ago' is true and inevitable. The Farewell to Beauty is made on a less anguished note, a note of resignation, and again

the cumulative effect is exactly right. The opening stanza is especially admirable:

'Let fall your golden showers, laburnum tree!
Break the gold caskets of your buds for me –
Soon I shall go where never gold is seen,
And who will be with you as I have been?'

The invocation is directed in the next stanza to
the 'silver bird' whose song was heard many
a day but soon shall be heard no more: then
comes, with excellent judgment, a stanza of
Omar Khayyám-like, impersonal reflectiveness,
followed by a return to the individual note:

'All things so early fade – swiftly pass over,
As autumn bees desert the withering clover.
Now, with the bee, I sing immortal June;
How soon both song and bee are gone—how
    soon!'

The most impressive feature of the poem, and
the important one from the standpoint of vision
and craftsmanship alike, is still to come. Of
course the theme, so far, has been used by
earlier poets on several occasions, and with such
perfection that any later poem in which it is
introduced must be challenged immediately,
notably by Matthew Arnold's lines –

'So, some tempestuous morn in early June,
  When the year's primal burst of bloom is
          o'er,
    Before the roses and the longest day –
When garden-walks, and all the grassy floor,
  With blossoms, red and white, of fallen
          May,
    And chestnut flowers are strewn –
So have I heard the cuckoo's parting cry,
  From the wet field, through the vext garden-
          trees,
    Come with the volleying rain and tossing
          breeze.
The bloom is gone, and with the bloom go I.'

Mary Webb's verses expressed, wistfully and with a greater simplicity than these of Matthew Arnold, the emotion of one who is numbed and bewildered for a single, immediate moment by the revelation that life goes on. But the human ego refuses to entertain it for longer than that first moment. It is rebellious, as always, against the prospect of life continuing without oneself being part of it in some personal survival. In the final verses this attitude causes a remarkable change in the atmosphere of the poem in order that the simple, questioning mind shall not be alone, the loneliness having served its purpose. We learn for the first time that the 'dreaming god' of Beauty has been present in the same scene. If Beauty deserts the scene, which it must to satisfy the ego, it will only do so, Beauty being immortal, in order that its presence might be transferred elsewhere. Thus comes the egoistic compromise. Where the dreaming god of Beauty goes there will the poet go also, and not only the state of nothingness be avoided, but also the laburnum tree, the silver bird, the bee, and all the rest will fade out, the thought of the persistence of anything else independently being as intolerable to the ego as the thought of its own destruction. So all is settled: therefore the scene will not remain either. But the departure does not mean extinction, for the dreaming god of Beauty is brought to the rescue. And the technique of the poem, in order that the early simplicity may be followed naturally by this complexity, develops into a relatively complicated series of word pictures.

'Who'll watch the clover secretly unclose?
Finger the sycamore buds, afire with rose?
Trace the mauve veins of the anemone?
Know the peculiar scent of every tree?

A Factory of Peace.

I watched her in the loud and shadowy lanes
Of life; and every face that passed her by
Grew calmly restful, smiling quietly
As though she gave, for all their griefs & pains
Largesse of comfort, soft as summer rains,
And balsam tinctured with tranquillity:
Yet in her own eyes dwelt an agony.
"Oh, halcyon soul!" I cried, "what sorrow reigns
In that calm heart which knows such ways to heal?"
She said — "Where balms are made for human uses,
Great furnace fires, and wheel on grinding wheel
Must crush and purify the crude herb juices;
And in some hearts the conflict cannot cease;
They are the sick world's factories of peace."

M. W.

A POEM BY MARY WEBB IN HER OWN HAND

'Maybe the solemn hill, the enchanted plain
Will be but arable and wild again,
Losing the purple bloom they wore for me –
The dreaming god I could so clearly see.'

Mary Webb's craftsmanship seldom becomes as subtle as it is in 'Farewell to Beauty.' For the most part she is content that it shall express simple emotions in simple terms. When the sonnet-form is used with a single aim, uncomplicated by even a passing 'aside,' the chances of success in that deceptive medium are made easier. Mary Webb heard a blackbird singing in London, and in the sonnet which she wrote as a consequence she unerringly concentrates on the first stabbing thought that rushes into a mind which is abnormally predisposed to it. In the strict sense 'To A Blackbird Singing in London' is not a sonnet at all, for most of the rules are violated – notably that there shall be a clear break between the octet and the sestet, nor is the rhyme-scheme accurate, for although the second, third, sixth, and seventh lines rhyme together, the first and fourth do not rhyme with the fifth and eighth.

Nevertheless, it may be considered as one of the poems that mark her highest accomplishment. And if, after reading it now, we recall it when we have followed the course of her life a little further, we shall perceive it to express the prevailing mood of her later maturity.

'Sing on, dear bird! Bring the old rapturous
     pain,
In this great town, where I no welcome find.
Show me the murmuring forest of your mind,
And April's fragile cups, brimful of rain.
Oh sing me far away, that I may hear
The voice of grass, and weeping, may be blind
To slights and lies and friends that prove
     unkind.
Sing till my soul dissolves into a tear,
Glimmering within a chaliced daffodil.
So, when the stately sun with burning breath
Absorbs my being, I'll dream that he is Death,
Great Death, the undisdainful. By his will
No more unlovely, haunting all things fair,
I'll seek some kinder life in the golden air.'

CHAPTER FOUR

She Becomes a Novelist and writes 'The Golden Arrow'

I

THE poems of Mary Webb were not gathered into a volume during her life. At one stage of her work she had definite plans about publishing them, and she even selected a general title for the collection. But the poems accumulated more and more slowly as time went on, and she was unable to make up her mind that she had written a number sufficient in bulk to justify such a harvesting. Many were printed in the periodicals, and now and again the editor of a new anthology sought her permission to reprint one or two examples in company with other contemporary work. Thus in *Come Hither*, his 'Collection of Rhymes and Poems for the Young of all ages,' Mr. Walter de la Mare included 'Green Rain' ('Into the scented woods we'll go'), 'The Water Ousel' ('Where on the wrinkled stream the willows lean'), and 'Market Day' ('Who'll walk the fields with us to town?'). And St. John Adcock chose 'An Old Woman' ('They bring her flowers'), and 'Foxgloves' ('The foxglove bells, with lolling tongue'), to represent her in his *Bookman Treasury of Living Poets*. Mr. Adcock's prefatory note to these two examples referred to her as 'a novelist who joins a subtle mastery of narrative and profound psychological insight, a grace and beauty of style which is a prevailing charm in her still uncollected poems.'

Not until after her death, therefore, was the collection finally completed and published. Her essays, on the other hand, were gathered by her into the volume *The Spring of Joy: a Little Book of Healing* during the years immediately preceding 1911, when she began to submit the manuscript to various publishers. Unsuccessfully, it must be added, although she received from more than one publisher a letter of appreciation. Eventually she lost her enthusiasm, and put the manuscript aside. Several years later she returned to it, and after making substantial alterations again approached the publishers. This time she was successful, and in 1917 *The Spring of Joy* was accepted by the firm of J. M. Dent & Son. It was not through this work, however, that she experienced an author's first and unique thrill of seeing his writing as a book, for *The Golden Arrow*, a novel, was published in the previous year.

It is rather ironical that as a volume *The Spring of Joy* should have sprung from sorrow. During the winter of 1909 Gladys Mary Meredith, as she was still, suffered the loss of her well-loved father – the father whom she saw in her creative mind as she portrayed John Arden in *The Golden Arrow*, whose face 'ran into kindly smiles as easily as a brook runs in its accustomed bed.' People did not mind John Arden laughing at them 'when they saw the endless charity of his eyes, wistful with his long gazing into unattainable beauty': he would break into 'the wholehearted laughter of an old man who has never wilfully done wrong or consciously done right; for he was lifted by his simple love of all creatures as far above right and wrong as his cottage was above the plain.'

The distress of this intimate encounter with death was acute. Time was to soften the sharpness, but we have more than one page of evidence in her writings afterwards that the hurt remained long after less sensitive natures would have been wholly salved. There is, especially, the passage in which Stephen the preacher (of *The Golden Arrow*)

'suddenly knew why he loved lights, colour, spring, song; why men built themselves warm houses, and planted orchards; why women made their windows bright with geraniums and clean muslin; why mothers delighted in their babies and young men delighted in football and the zest of love. It was because all these things kept away the idea of death – the knowledge of future intimacy with it; because they built up around the fleeting moment the sapphire walls of immortality.'

And because Gladys Mary Meredith was not one who could easily dismiss the thought of death, the consequences were serious. Soon after her father had been laid away in the old churchyard at Ightfield, near Whitchurch, on the northern border of the county, her malady of eight years earlier returned, and it was a very delicate young woman who, in January, 1911, met her future husband at Corner Cottage, the house in Meole Brace of a neighbour, Miss Southern, who remembers Mary Webb as uncommonly clever in talking and writing. 'She could sit down and write a first-class essay

straight away on any subject you set her,'
declares Miss Southern – 'and I know what
that means, for I was once a school-mistress.'
She was also a clever bridge-player. Often
Mary joined at a hand of bridge in Miss Southern's parlour. 'She was an invalid longer than
she ought to have been,' adds Miss Southern,
'she was so active, mentally and physically, that
she got no proper rest when she was ill.'

II

Mr. Henry Bertram Law Webb and Gladys
Mary Meredith were married in 1912 at
Meole Brace Parish Church. She was then a
woman of thirty-one, with brown hair and un-
usually prominent blue eyes. Her expression
was habitually cheery, and she had a busy life
in spite of her temporary frailness. She was
an active member of the Church of England,
being a Communicant and a district visitor.
The books she studied at that period, her
husband remembers, made a deep impression
on her: their titles are significant, especially in
view of the reaction that ensued: *Divine Revelations, The Meditations of Mother Julian of
Norwich, Consolations of the Divine Love.* Ere

long the pagan *Story of My Heart* by Richard Jefferies was bulking more largely in her mind, and during her later years, although she never put aside her Bible, of which she had a wide and profound knowledge, she studied the poetry of Robert Browning, which helped her when orthodox religion ceased to be a potent influence. But even then, Mr. Webb recalls, 'she was more interested in birds and flowers than in books. When I met her she was a thoroughly normal-minded person. Her normality, indeed, affected one like the enlightenment and sensibility of someone in an outlandish part of the countryside whom one doesn't expect to find there.'

The dedication of Mary Webb's first novel is to her husband. The dedication of her last novel is also to her husband. Thus the durability of their union is commemorated. She found happiness in her marriage. Mr. Webb, whose uncle was the famous pioneer of Channel swimming, Captain Matthew Webb, had been a graduate at Cambridge University, and he was also a native of her own Shropshire. At the time of their first acquaintance he was a schoolmaster in Shrewsbury, after an earlier term at Leeds, Yorkshire. The unconventionality of outlook that was shared by them may be deduced from a passage in *Gone to Earth* that conveys its extreme opposite: 'The everlasting tyranny of the material over the abstract; of bluster over nerves; strength over beauty; states over individuals; churches over souls; and fox-hunting squires over the creatures they honour with their attention.'

This unconventionality developed freely, and an occurrence prior to their marriage illustrates it. Mary Webb became very ill, and for three weeks lay in a delirium of an uncommon kind, but had a medical specialist been called to her he would doubtless have saved her from its recurrence later in life. Mr. Webb was a constant visitor to the sickroom, and in desperation, after many restless days and nights, she demanded that he should take over the duties of nurse. Straightway an improvement in her condition showed itself, and tended by him unceasingly, she was quickly well enough for her wedding day.

'The grave beautiful day,' she called one such day in *The House in Dormer Forest*: the grave beautiful day on which

'all beautiful things seemed to run to meet her.

Already there had come the faint dusking-over of the wheatfields with the soft rosy fawn which steals away the green of summer; which glows and flushes through hot days and yellow-moon nights until at last, through every phase of saffron, tawny, almost salmon-colour, they have reached the time when they can hold no more beauty. The ripples that swept over them, water-green and pale when the first clover flowered, now flowed in a slower rhythm, each wave longer and stiffer, less like water than honey.

'She thought, as her gaze lingered on the plain, that there a shadow wavered which was not painted by any tree, slipping away before the eye of man like dew from a lifted leaf. It seemed, as she looked ahead at some green-veiled arch of the forest, that the curtain might be twitched aside at any moment, and some revelation of the divine peer out upon her. But when she passed the archway there was only the leafy, mazy pattern of summer green. As she listened to the low breathing of the forest, she half-thought she heard an echo fall – like the striking of a wing on soft resistant air, or the music of wild swans passing above the roof of cloud, sounding upon their muffled golden gongs. . . .'

Elsewhere too she commemorates 'the grave beautiful day':

'In her short life there had not been many moments of such rose and gold. It was the happiest hour of *his* life also; for she looked to him as flowers to warm heaven, as winter birds to a fruited tree.' . . . 'She stood in the immortal company of those that have it in their power to give joy and do not miss their chance, crowning the beloved early with untarnished gold and morning flowers. . . . "What else matters?" she thought.' . . .

The experiences of Amber Darke and Hazel Woodus and Deborah Arden in her novels were an imaginative counterpart of her own spiritual experience at her bridal in the village church a few hundred yards distant from 'Maesbrook,' her home at Meole Brace. To say that the setting of that marriage was picturesque is more advisable than to say it was venerable, for the church, a building of red sandstone, was erected as recently as in 1869, being the third that has stood there. Nevertheless, the surroundings of worn, green-stained tombstones and ivy-twined trees, in which the rooks are busy and noisy year after year, convey a sense of age, especially when we envision the bright wedding procession that approached along the leafy, wandering lane bounded by a mellow red-brick wall on one side, and the rural view that spreads wide on the other side – a view which maybe drew the bride's eyes past the vicarage buildings to the modern cemetery in the distance behind the churchyard, the cemetery of white graves where Mary Webb rests now with all her gifts and memories.

III

Hazel Woodus, the most lovable of all Mary Webb's heroines, was endowed with a whimsicality that flashed forth at moments so unexpected as to be disconcerting. It was a quality that her creator shared, as her relatives and friends at Meole Brace were made to realize at the marriage ceremony. For Gladys Mary Meredith, as we now call her for the last time, 'chose for her guests the inmates of the women's ward of the workhouse she visited; an old herbalist who had endeared himself to her by his knowledge of plants; a poor old fellow who only possessed one sound eye; and a decrepit organ grinder.'

So began a wedded life that lasted fifteen years, and was only ended by her death. Straightway after the ceremony, carrying away the blessing of her widowed mother and a not entirely negligible allowance which it is as well for us to remember at certain moments in her life-story yet to come, Mr. and Mrs. H. B. L. Webb left for Weston-super-Mare, where he was to pursue his scholastic duties for the next two years. They had no liking for the place. 'We were two people,' says Mr. Webb, 'who felt at home in old clothes, corduroys, or, in Mary's case, a faded sunbonnet. The people of Weston-super-Mare would have felt far from home in them.'

Nevertheless, that seaside resort on the coast of Somerset is important in Mary Webb's career, because it was there that, concentrating on a treasured volume of Shropshire folk-lore she had taken with her, she came to know that she could never live happily except in her own county; and there, moreover, she made the tentative beginnings of her first novel, *The Golden Arrow*.

IV

Mary Webb was a whole decade in becoming a novelist. One of the most discerning and sympathetic appraisers of her work has described her as 'a writer by choice and a novelist by chance,' and assuredly she groped her way rather than leaped towards the vantage-ground from which life could be surveyed as a whole and her perception of it given ampler expression than that of essay and verse.

Her realization that the novel was the suitable medium for this ampler expression had swift results. At the end of their two-years' sojourn in a house at Weston-super-Mare the Webbs returned to Shropshire, and made their first home at Rose Cottage, Pontesbury, a village lying ten miles south-west of Shrewsbury. Rose Cottage is a tiny modern villa (since re-named Roseville) and it is withdrawn by a stone's throw from the main roadway and the modest railway station. There it was that she gathered together the notes for a novel which she had begun to make in Somerset.

Gathering inspiration and momentum during the spring of 1915, she announced, one summer morning too wet for work in the garden, that she felt inclined to write something of a new character. Three weeks later she showed her husband the completed first manuscript of *The Golden Arrow*.

There are approximately a hundred thousand words in *The Golden Arrow*. She must have written five or six thousand a day: we are told that 'her thoughts flowed.' Indeed they flowed so swiftly that her husband found it necessary to procure a special kind of fountain-pen for her, one that supplied its ink with accelerated speed. Nearly always after that the actual transference of her thoughts and ideas was rapid. It was spasmodic as well. She had no regular hours of writing. Nor were her household duties allowed to distract her. They were not neglected, of course, particularly as she fulfilled them without paid help, but once she turned from her cooking and settled down with her pen and paper she was heedless of all interruption short of such alarms as the smell of burning. And when her day's writing was read over for possible revision she usually found that her most quickly-composed passages were the best. They required little or no correction. 'The pages most typical in her manuscripts,' we are told, 'have the fewest changes.'

v

Once Mary Webb felt impelled to shape her writing into that first novel she did not hesitate to begin the story straight away, and unlike the leisurely pastoral novelists who were her contemporaries, or approximately contemporaries, such as Thomas Hardy and Eden Phillpotts, she preferred to interweave her description of the setting with the actions of her characters, rather than, for introductory purposes, keep it separate. Compare, for example, the beginning of one of Hardy's novels – not *The Return of the Native*, in which the picture of Egdon Heath occupies the whole first chapter before 'Humanity Comes on the Scene,' for in this instance the profound influence of the heath over the human renders it inevitable – but the novel which *The Golden Arrow* most nearly resembles in scope and purpose: *The Woodlanders*. The villagers in *The Woodlanders* are illuminated by the subtle influence of their

112

surrounding woods: the villagers of *The Golden Arrow* are drenched with what Mr. G. K. Chesterton describes (in his introduction to the novel in the Collected Edition) as 'that mysterious light in which solid things become semi-transparent. It is a light not shining on things, but through them.' When a figure moves in that Shropshire setting it is not immediately that we perceive it to be old John Arden, or the young Deborah, Lily or Joe. It is as much a part of earth as though it were 'a tree walking.'

The setting itself is presented in lovely fragments, such as that which brings before us the famous Devil's Chair, a 'mass of quartzite blackened and hardened by uncountable ages,' towering in 'gigantic aloofness' above the range of hills known as the Stiperstones, in the south-west corner of the county. The village of Pontesbury rests against the northern shoulder of the Stiperstones, which is Nills Hill, so that Mary Webb wrote the novel directly under the influence of this five-miles-long range from which may be viewed the Severn Valley, the Wenlocks, the Stretton Hills, and, moreover, the Welsh Hills as far as Snowdon. Indeed, John Arden's stone cottage in which, on the first page of the story, his daughter Deborah is discovered washing dishes, is the prototype of the farm-house to which, during 1916, the increased cost of living in the war-years led Mr. and Mrs. Webb from Rose Cottage. The rent of 'The Nills' was £13 a year, that of Rose Cottage had been £36.

These figures indicate the remoteness, if not the loneliness, of the farm-house. It stands a mile away from Pontesbury, towards the hills, along a road which breaks into half a dozen winding, hedge-lined laneways where the only sounds are of children playing, hoofs clattering, and birds singing. The track which leads past 'The Nills' farm-house fords a pebbly stream, passes an inn with a sign which advertises 'Wem Ales' and also a post-box which is inscribed 'V. R.' and hung on the fence of a cottage garden. As you walk along this road 'The Nills' might easily escape you, for it stands back fifty yards and is hidden by trees, so that only chimney-smoke betrays it. For artistic purposes the situation of the house was rearranged when Mary Webb made use of it in her first novel (written before she ever stepped inside it).

'While washing dishes Deborah could see,

through the small age-misted pane, counties and blue ranges lying beneath the transparent or hazy air in the bright, unfolding beauty of inviolate nature. She would gaze out between the low window-frame and the lank geraniums, forgetting the half-dried china, when grey rain-storms raced across from far Cader Idris, ignoring in their majestic progress the humble, variegated plains of grass and grain, breaking like a tide on the unyielding heather and the staunch cottage. Beyond the kitchen and attached to the house was the shippen, made of weather-boarding, each plank overlapping the next. This was lichen-grey, like the house, stone and wood having become worn as the hill-folk themselves, browbeaten and mellowed by the tempestuous years, yet tenacious, defying the storm. Sitting in the kitchen on a winter night, the Ardens could hear the contented rattle of the two cow-chains from the shippen, the gentle coughing and stamping of the folded sheep, . . . and now and then a hill pony — strayed from the rest — whickered through the howling ferocity of the gale.'

Such is 'The Nills' as it has become at the hands of the artist when the curtain rises in

The Golden Arrow. Thenceforward the place is dominated by the theme, which is love. Not the love of man for woman, but that of rare womanhood in all times, bestowed upon mates usually unworthy of it in spirit and body, mates unable to respond with love on the same plane. In the consequent disillusion and suffering is the tragic irony of life, and the bitterest aspect is in the woman's knowledge that the agent of disillusionment and suffering is not even remotely aware of what is happening to the sufferer. The tragedy, as Mary Webb presents it, is fittingly enacted within sight of 'the long mammothlike shape of Diafol Mountain,' for a more callous and ruthless environment could not have been chosen:

' "It's raining over the Devil's Chair now," said Deborah.
'On the highest point of the bare, opposite ridge, now curtained in driving storm-cloud, towered in gigantic aloofness a mass of quartzite, blackened and hardened by uncountable ages. In the plain this pile of rock and the rise on which it stood above the rest of the hill-top would have constituted a hill in itself. The scattered rocks, the ragged holly-brakes on the

lower slopes were like small carved lions beside the black marble steps of a stupendous throne.

'Nothing ever altered its look. Dawn quickened over it in pearl and emerald; summer sent the armies of heather to its very foot; snow rested there as doves nest in cliffs. It remained inviolable, taciturn, evil. It glowered darkly on the dawn; it came through the snow like jagged bones through flesh; before its hardness even the venturesome cranberries were discouraged. For miles around, in the plains, the valleys, the mountain dwellings, it was feared.

'It drew the thunder, people said. Storms broke round it suddenly out of a clear sky; it seemed almost as if it created storm. No one cared to cross the range near it after dark — when the black grouse laughed sardonically and the cry of a passing curlew shivered like broken glass. The sheep that inhabited these hills would, so the shepherds said, cluster suddenly and stampede for no reason, if they had grazed too near it in the night.

'So the throne stood, bleak, massive, untenanted, yet with a well-worn air. It had the look of a chair from which the occupant has just risen, to which he will shortly return. It was understood that only when vacant could the throne be seen. Whenever rain, sleet or mist made a grey shechinah there people said, "There's harm brewing." "He's in his chair." Not that they talked of it much; they simply felt it, as sheep feel the coming of snow.'

In this environment is enacted the story of Deborah Arden's disillusionment. Deborah is the first of Mary Webb's bewildered girls struggling through misunderstanding and inner perplexity to a dimly apprehended spiritual refuge. 'She had her code, she had summed up life; marriage and all its cares, griefs and joys came into her sum of things.' But passion was different, strange and terrible. That it would assail her and what it involved, she knew not. We see her in the beginning as a girl 'very straight and gracious in the blue delaine,' the 'tower-like hillsides' a mere background for her, the colours grouping themselves behind her 'like meek waiting maids.' We see her 'standing like the goddess of some rich land.' But to that lonely part of the world comes Stephen Southernwood, the wandering preacher, tall, with ruffled hair of gold, 'excited blue eyes, bright colour and radiant bearing,' 'ludicrously unsuited to his black clothes.'

With the rest of the Arden family she attends his service, and after a time Deborah found herself kneeling with crimson cheeks, no breath, and the knowledge that she could not look at the preacher.

' "What's come over me?" she whispered to herself. She secretly mopped her face and the palms of her hands. . . . She felt a gathering sense of desolation which, if she had been able to analyse her emotions, she would have known to arise from a new sense of dependency – a disturbance of poise. Towards the end of the service the growling in the east changed to a roar; rain came like a high tide on the black windows; the young preacher stood in a flicker of lightning as though he were haloed for glory or smitten for doom.'

The alternative consequences of such love as that which is quick to awaken in Deborah are in this symbolistic phrase, 'haloed for glory or smitten for doom.' For Stephen Southernwood, the first of Mary Webb's men characters complementary to that array of young women, is also bewildered, he also is struggling towards some vaguely desired refuge of the spirit. That the struggle is unsuccessful in his case is

Deborah's tragedy. 'Had he loved Deborah with all his being they would have been safe. But he loved in the manner of many civilized people, and not in Deborah's way.' An incident at the merry-go-round illustrates the division between them.

'Stephen's eyes were ablaze. He loved quick motion, music, colour. He had an arm round Deborah, and the more excited he was the more like iron it grew.

' "Oh, Stephen!" she pleaded; "loose me go!"

'But he was beside himself with excitement, the fulfilment of his emotional and poetic love of beauty, and crude life.

' "I won't," he said.

' "O, do 'ee, Stephen! You're hurting me."

'The merry-go-round was in full swing, racing madly, the music at its loudest and quickest.

'He bent down.

' "Deb," he shouted, with his mouth close to her ear, his eyes holding hers, dominant, flashing blue fire: "Deb – when?"

' "You're hurting me, Stephen."

' "Then say!"

' "Oh, Stephen – and you said you were fond of me."

' "I tell you it's *because* I'm fond of you." He spoke in a hard voice, holding her tighter. His logic seemed unanswerable to him. He was without Joe's dumb apologies for the ways of nature. His arm never slackened, though the tune did. He had no idea where he was; he was so intent on his desire.

' "Say when!" he repeated.

' "I dunna know what you mean."

' "That's a lie." '

Deborah needed time to fuse the two fires, to realize that in unity there was only purity. But she realizes it too late. Stephen betrays her love, first by deserting her, then through an association, trivial but significant, with Deborah's sister-in-law, Lily, who is married to Joe Arden. The story of Joe and Lily runs alongside that of Stephen and Deborah, and the skill of an already matured craftsman is in the contrast of their futures in love and wedlock, made with an ebb-and-flow movement – ebbing in the case of Stephen and Deborah when it flows in that of Joe and Lily, the grossness of the situation in which the two last-named are the central figures being invariably emphasized precisely when the subtlety of the situation of Stephen and Deborah requires explanation, an explanation which Mary Webb's excellent intuition knows will be the more valuable for being indirect. Sometimes the contrast is made by bringing one of each of the two pairs together.

'"Stephen's not 'a man'," (declared the newly-married Deborah to the newly-married Lily). "He's *my* man. And he's my lad and my friend." . . . She searched for a way of making Lily understand. "And the lover of my soul," she concluded.

'"That's blasphemy, Deborah. It's a hymn."

'"If your man inna the lover of your soul," said Deborah, "you've missed the honey and only got the empty comb. . . . I'm thinking it's only then as you've a right to be called his wife and sleep along of him."

'"You talk very indecent, Deborah, to my thinking."

'"It inna talking straight that's indecent; it's smiling and sniggering and colouring up over things." '

The character of Joe, Lily's husband, is

emphasized by his mother. He is strangely different from his father, John Arden, and his sister Deborah, but easily accounted for as one of the same family through his mother, crude in all her ways, though in Mary Webb's portrait not by any means unredeemed. 'The more she loved people the more tart Mrs. Arden was, until her husband used to say ruefully that he wished she was a bit more callous-like to him, for he felt like a pickled damson.' When Mrs. Arden needs to raise her voice she is described as shrieking – although the occasion may be utterly matter-of-fact, unemotional: – ' "Deb!" shrieked Mrs. Arden up the breakneck stairs, "take the tray and ring up Joe, there's a good girl." '

Elsewhere 'she raised her voice and put a twist on it so that it might negotiate the crooked stairs.'

Joe is loutish, earthy, and the problems of his relationship with Lily are all a 'jumblement' to him, as he puts it, 'like them anthems when they try who'll sing fastest.' But he is honest and blissfully trustful that somehow they will become 'clear as the Christmas star.' Lily also is explained by her parent, Eli Huntbatch, a widower, a man 'with no honey in his heart' as

John Arden says, and for whom even his daughter loses human feeling. The character of Eli, and the attitude of those around him to his meanness, and callousness, is vividly exposed when the lambs, feeling an aura about Deborah, pressed round her, and

' "Dirty beasts!" said Eli, sweeping them back with his stick. "Not but what that black 'un will bring a good price come Christmas."

' "Dunna clout 'em, Eli!" came John's voice from the threshold. "I'd liefer they'd come round me than find the pot of gold under the rainbow. They be my friends, as you know well, and they'm not speechless from emptiness of heart. No, sorrowful and loving they be!"

' "Meat, that's what they be," said Eli.

' "Deb!" whispered Lily, "isn't he an old beast? I hate him more every day, and I wish I could get married, that I do!" '

Lily is presented, not without sympathy, as the embodiment of spurious love, as possessing a 'passionless breast'; one who acts always

'with the complete absorption in her own small, superficial ego in face of great primeval powers which makes a certain type of woman the slave of sex instead of the handmaid of love. She was what is called a good girl, thinking no worse thoughts than the crude ones of most farm women. She was insatiably curious. . . . She was full of tremors and flushes – the livery of passion – yet incapable of understanding passion's warm self. She was ready to give herself as a woman for the sake of various material benefits, with a pathetic ignorance of her own unthinkable worth as a human being. She was rapacious for the small-change of sex, yet she would never be even stirred by the agony of absence from the beloved.'

VI

Thus the stage is set for the drama of *The Golden Arrow*, –

'We have sought it, we have sought the golden
    arrow
  (Bright the sally-willows sway)
Two and two by paths low and narrow,
  Arm-in-crook along the mountain way.
  Break o' frost and break o' day!
Some were sobbing through the gloom
When we found it, when we found the golden
    arrow –
  Wand of willow in the secret cwm.'

The drama is one of major tragedy and minor tragedy. The minor tragedy, that of Joe and Lily, is rounded off with a superficial happiness. Joe has desired 'to have little 'uns sitting around with their mugs – I thought to have six – ' and Lily, who thought mainly of the pain of having the six and the trouble of washing the mugs, has sought in a sordid, secret way to thwart that desire. His discovery of her selfishness and deceit precipitated a crisis. In her fear she capitulates. 'I'll let you off the other five,' he says regretfully, seeing his dream-picture fading. And stroking her hair, –

'   "What'll I be this time next year, Lil?" he whispered.

'   "A donkey," said Lil. . . .

'   "Gi's a kiss!" said Joe, who was tired with unwonted emotion, but happy, because in some mysterious way Lily was dearer than ever before.

'Lily was happy also, but quite untired, for emotion had as little effect on her as rain on a plant under glass – neither breaking nor renewing.'

The episode of Joe Arden and his Lily ends with the significant comment: 'Neither Lily nor

Joe . . . noticed that their respective weakness, doggedness, lack of principle, plethora of principle, tragedy and comedy, had left things just as they were: that with their will or without it the courses of life flowed on to their undreamed-of endings, from their mysterious source.'

Perhaps Deborah, as the major tragedy fades out, notices this – that things were left just as they had been. How could she, always discerning, when she has learnt her lesson, preternaturally acute by the time she has come through her suffering – how could Deborah fail to observe that the courses of life were flowing on without change, 'on to their un-dreamed-of endings, from their mysterious source'? When Stephen Southernwood deserts her she sits like a thing of stone in her mother's house all through the months of waiting, not for his return, but for the coming of her child. She is always willing to do her share of the home duties, but nothing gives her life, she neither smiles nor weeps. Only her father, John Arden, the most beautiful of all Mary Webb's creations – and when we remember who was the inspiration in her portrayal of him, this seems very fitting – is able to rouse Deborah, but the response she makes to him is hardly perceptible. Even when the child is born she does not become the joyous mother. But one day, as she wanders with her baby in the fields, she sees that 'The Devil's Chair had a light behind it from the setting sun: rays came from it as if it had a heart of warmth. Suddenly, in the grave silence of all things at sundown, Deborah turned sharply as if at a cry.' A man had appeared walking with the difficult haste of one eager but exhausted. It was Stephen, the husband who had failed and deserted her. The scene which follows is humanly poignant, artistically inspiriting.

'You'm tired, lad,' she says with quick concern, and he answers, 'Not now. I was. But now I'm home.'

But Deborah did not understand. Too much pain had left her bewildered, misunderstandings arose, as they inevitably would in such a situation unless the actors are patient, and empty in their hearts of all but mutual sympathy and a passion for peace. Deborah misunderstands his lack of interest in the child he has only now seen for the first time. She did not realize that he was thinking only of her. . . . And so in a swift stroke they are divided again. Stephen makes a last plea.

' "Deborah! Live with me once more – just for one week, one day, at home yonder above Lostwithin. You'll understand then," he cried frantically; "you'll know without telling when you see how I'll take care of you!"

' "There inna no whome there now, for I burnt the things. And the cattle go to and agen by the hearth. And there's none to stay the wind and the rain driving in o'er the thrashold."

' "I'll make a new home; I can!" He flung his head back with his old unconquerable look.

' "Thank you kindly, Stephen, but I'm well enough as I be. It's only your goodheartedness, I know. But I dunna need to be beholden to anyone."

' "But it's I that would be beholden, Deborah. I'm asking it as a favour, the greatest in the world."

' "Afore, when you asked, I gave you all I had – such as it was; and you flung it back in my face. I've no ill-feeling, Stephen. Only I've no more to give."

'Stephen stood up. On his face as he looked down at her was the lambent beauty of those who find the Golden Arrow and clasp it to their hurt and glory. His face was the face of her dream. In the dusk, tall and deep-eyed beside the little signpost, he was the incarnation of the Flockmaster.

'Worn, world-battered, despairing, he stood there in a grandeur that had not been his before – the splendour of perfect manhood. All the passions of his larger nature were quelled before this new burning force in him. All his old readiness of tongue, his old poses, were gone.

'He felt nothing of his own tragic beauty as he said gently –

' "The dew's falling, Deb. You two should be home. Good-night."

' "Good-night, Stephen," said Deborah, not realizing the parting any more than the meeting; "and may the kindly light be along with you."

* * *

'As soon as he was out of sight, all power of movement left Deborah. There was no room in her mind for anything but the sense that her fingers had touched his hair, and now did not touch it. Slowly, as life comes back to a paralysed limb, she awoke to the knowledge that he had been here and was gone. What did it matter whether he loved her or not, whether she was a "kept woman" or not, whether he left her again some day? She wanted him. Everything else was washed from her brain by this primeval, ungovernable passion for the reassurance of touch.

'She hastily put the child in the heather, though it was wet with dew. Even motherhood was swept away. She ran along the path calling "Stephen! Stephen!"''

The faithful John Arden, faithful to ideals as well as to reality, is the hero of the final chapter. Searching the hills through the night, while Deborah and her mother sit waiting in the cosy kitchen at the farm, he finds Stephen. But Southernwood, symbol of humanity running blindly down a steep towards its refuge, suddenly stands in the doorway alone. When John Arden arrives a little later, the old man explains: ' "The lad outstripped me, Mother. I'm thinking it's the shippen for you and me to-night, while cut love's mending." '

And the chapter ends with John speaking again, a large glory about his memory as the reader closes the book. His wife has asked if Deborah and Stephen need fire and lamp, and he answers: ' "D'you mind the tale of them that found the Golden Arrow, and went with apple-blow scent around them, and a mort o' bees, and warmship, and wanted naught of any man? There's no need of fire or candle for them, my dear, for they'm got their light – the kindly light – and the thorn's white over." '

Except in the matter of craftsmanship, which is perfected only with experience, Mary Webb did but one thing better in her career as novelist than *The Golden Arrow*, this tragedy of lovers who sought that emblem of true love, and after they found it, 'clung to it fast though it met wound them sore. And nought will part 'em, neither in the flower of life nor in the brown winrow.'

CHAPTER FIVE

'*Gone To Earth*' – *in* '*a World So Black With Hate*'

I

DURING the period in which Mary Webb and her husband lived at Pontesbury the tragedy of the World War was intensified. Down in that remote Shropshire village of queer insignificant coal-mines and lead-mines pricking the heart of agricultural country-land, 'the rumours and alarms of war at hand and danger pressing nigh' were as profound an influence as they were in the nation's capital, two hundred miles away. Mr. John Masefield's poem, 'August 1914,' from which we have just taken a phrase, shows most vividly what the war signified in the minds of the men and women who dwelt away in English hills and valleys, among –

'these fields where evening drives
Beauty like breath, so gently darkness falls.
Darkness that makes the meadows holier still,'

in 'this quiet scene' of 'the lone Downland' with the forlorn woods 'loved to the death, inestimably dear.' It signified to the very humblest of those Shropshire villagers,

'The breaking off of ties, the loss of friends,
Death, like a miser getting in his rent,
And no new stones laid where the trackway ends.'

It signified

'The harvest not yet won, the empty bin,
The friendly horses taken from the stalls,
The fallow on the hill not yet brought in,
The cracks unplastered in the leaking walls.'

They heard the news, the men labouring on the hillside near Mary Webb's home at Rose Cottage or 'The Nills,' they heard it exactly as the men of another county did in Mr. Masefield's poem, who –

'Went discouraged home,
And brooded by the fire with heavy mind,
With such dumb loving of the Berkshire loam
As breaks the dumb hearts of the English kind,
Then sadly rose and left the well-loved Downs,
And so by ship to sea and knew no more
The fields of home, the buyers, the market towns,
Nor the dear outline of the English shore. . . .'

The influence of the war on Mary Webb was more than usually acute. Her three brothers, Kenneth, Douglas, and Mervyn, had gone as soldiers overseas, and the loneliness and terror were aggravated by the absence of her sister Muriel in Gibraltar. She wrote regularly to each of them, and when the news came that Mervyn Meredith, who had joined up from Keble College, Oxford, was badly wounded, her concern for her favourite 'Duss,' who eventually became a captain in the Royal Artillery and won the Military Cross, led her to write almost the only poem directly concerned with what she called 'a world so black with hate.' 'The Lad Out There' is an appeal to the Powers of Love, 'if still you lean above a world so black with hate,' to bring him –

'Whatever he may be or do
While absent far beyond my call,
Bring him, the long day's march being through,
Safe home to me some evenfall.'

The bitterness that all genuinely creative artists must instinctively feel when the forces of destruction are rampant was hers, just as sorrow was hers also. More than ever she felt that the only salvation of the loving heart lay near the earth. Her worst fears about humanity when it is estranged from earth had been realized. Moreover, it was Nature alone that could shed calm upon our scarlet wars, as she wrote in another poem 'A Night Sky (1916)' – it was the moon that, 'beyond her violet bars from towering heights of thunder-cloud,' soothed 'a world so small, so loud.' Otherwise the loving heart was desolate 'as it hath ever been.' Thus she revealed her suffering spirit.

In two characteristic ways she sought her own relief. The war had affected her material position adversely: her husband, handicapped through ill-health, was now earning a hand-to-mouth living by coaching a few pupils, but the Webbs depended mainly on the small annual allowance that she received, in common with her brothers and sisters, from her widowed mother, who had gone to live at Chester since the death of Mr. Meredith. Mary Webb was not temperamentally equipped for economies, and as the cost of living increased she and her husband became very poor indeed. It occurred to her, therefore, that a little additional money might be made through the sale of the flowers and fruit in their garden at Rose Cottage.

Not only for the sake of the money, though,

did she seek to put the idea into practice, but because she would thereby regain her old close touch with the good earth. At first she supplied her produce to stall-holders in Shrewsbury Market, but soon she sought and secured a stall for herself. And recalling the little experiment, about which so much has been written, her husband describes how they would rise at three o'clock in the morning, and gather the fresh flowers. Then, leaving him to visit the houses in the locality and offer apples on a barrow, she proceeded to walk the nine miles from Pontesbury to Shrewsbury in order to take her stand in the market. She offered roses and other blooms at a halfpenny a bunch, and, says Mr. Webb, 'although I don't think she earned more than five shillings before she set out in the evening on the nine miles' walk home she was never dissatisfied. Indeed she came back looking much brighter: she felt she had done something beautiful.' She was like her own Abel Woodus in the next novel she was to write. 'All his means of livelihood were joys to him. He had the art of perpetual happiness in this, that he could earn as much as he needed by doing the work he loved.'

That the social standing of the Webbs

should suffer in the opinion of Pontesbury when their neighbours learnt of the venture was perhaps inevitable. 'She was nothing when she lived here,' was the comment of a man in charge of a local tradesman's cart when, a dozen years later, she was recalled to his memory. But Mary Webb was not in the least perturbed by the attitude of her neighbours. Walking and marketing sufficed, and she forgot all else. She was a splendid walker, and often she and her husband tramped twenty hilly miles towards Church Stretton, returning white with dust or soaked through with a storm that had surprised them. And to walk the country roads and the fields again, sometimes in the company of Mr. Webb, and sometimes alone; clad 'in an old coat and a faded gown,' seeing all around her the flowers and birds; 'the mower in the half-mown leasur' sipping his tea and taking his pleasure; meeting slow waggons ambling along the lane; watching the 'sad-eyed calves,' the foal 'playing in the grasses cool,' the startled lapwings, and the blackbird singing 'without fear where honeysuckle horns blow clear,' and coming at last with 'roots and country sweets' to Shrewsbury's steep old street as

> 'Golden bells and silver chimes
> Ring up and down the sleepy times' –

very lightheartedly she commemorated every moment of it in her poem 'Market Day'; to do all this, and on the journey home to see the dark blue hills away to the west and to guide her steps by the jagged hill that faces the Pontesbury village, and by the soft cottage lights shining out with a welcome – to do all this was to do more than find balm for her spiritual suffering, it was to feel her artistic power urged on to new labours. It may even be believed that the real reason why Mary Webb set up that stall in Shrewsbury Market was the novelist's subconscious pretext.

II

She stood at her brightly coloured stall in the spacious old Market Hall, glass-walled, glass-roofed, just off Shrewsbury's steep main street, surrounded by

'fruit from deep orchards by lost lanes, from the remote hills; flowers from gardens far from any high road; treasures of the wild in generous baskets, all piled in artless confusion – cheeses from the dairies beside the great meres;

white-frilled mushrooms from pastures where owl and weasel live undisturbed; generous roughly cut slabs of honeycomb from a strain of bees that were in these parts when Glendower came by; ducks with sage under their wings, as a lady carries her umbrella. . . .'

Certainly Mary Webb saw all this with the eye of the mind, as Mr. Baldwin has written, 'a mingling of peoples and traditions and turns of speech and proverbial wisdom that fostered in her memory and was fashioned for us in the little parcel of novels which is her legacy to literature.'

When Gideon and Prue Sarn, of *Precious Bane*, went to market their experience is described all the more graphically because of Mary Webb's own marketing experience – an experience that in the novel is enriched by her recollection of the town square, which, even to-day, when it is visited by scarlet motor-omnibuses, and taxi-cabs awaiting their fares under a statue of Clive, has an air of sleepiness and timelessness that lingers among the very stones of the grey buildings, especially where an old gabled shop leans out at the south corner. Above the entrance to one of the buildings there is an effigy supposed to represent a man in armour, and the accompanying inscription informs us that it had been transferred there by order of the Mayor from the 'Tower of the Welsh Bridge' in 1791. Another inscription records that: 'The XV day of June 1596, was this Buylding began by William Jones and Thomas Charlton Gent, then Bayliffes, and was erected and covered in their time.' The market known to readers of *Precious Bane* was a composite place that linked up the Market Hall and this Town Square:

'The market was in the open, in a paven square by the church. Each had his own booth, and the cheeses stood in mounds between. There were a sight of old women in decent shawls and cotton bonnets selling the same as we had, butter and eggs and poultry. There was a stall for gingerbread and one for mincepies. There was a sunbonnet stall, and a toy stall, and one for gewgaws such as strings of coral and china cats, shoe buckles and amulets and beaded reticules. It was a merry scene, with the bright holly and mistletoe, the cheeses yellow in the sun, and the gingerbread as brown and sticky as chestnut buds.

141

'The butcher stood at his door, which gave on to the market-place, shouting his meat, and holding up a long, shining knife, enough to make you think the French were coming. There was a woman selling hot potatoes and pig's fry, and a crockman who put up his wares to auction, and every time the clock chimed he broke summat, keeping some "*seconds*" in readiness, which served to amuse the people. Then the mummers came along and gave us a treat, and in one corner the beast-leech was pulling teeth out for a penny each, and had a crowd watching. What with them all shouting, and the mummers mouthing their parts, and the crash of broken china, and beasts lowing and bleating from the fair ground close by, and the chimes ringing out very sweet at the half-hours, you may think there was a cheerful noise.'

III

It was not long before Mary Webb's marketing days came to an end. No sooner had Rose Cottage been given up for The Nills farmhouse than her husband secured more lucrative schoolmastering at Chester. Although they mainly lived there during the summer of

1916, they contrived to return each week-end to Pontesbury. By this time Mary Webb was at the beginning of another novel, but she was made so miserable and low of heart by the prevailing distress and anxiety of the war and her acute sense of being a stranger to the Cheshire city that she had no heart for writing while she was away from her own county. Not even the publication of *The Golden Arrow*, which took place at that time, could give her the strength and desire to write: but as she crossed into Shropshire on Friday after-noons a remarkable new spirit seized upon her, and she would be in an exalted mood by the time they arrived at The Nills Farm. No sooner had she crossed the threshold than she sat down and wrote. Again she wrote at great speed. *The Golden Arrow* had been written in a few brief weeks, and before many of these weekends had passed, all of them devoted en-tirely to her new work of fiction, she gave 'To Him Whose Presence is Home,' as the dedica-tion reads, the first completed manuscript of her second novel, *Gone to Earth*. The final re-visions were not concluded until the following January, 1917, when the book was sent to the firm of Constable, who had published *The*

Golden Arrow. And in the same year, through these publishers, appeared *Gone to Earth*.

IV

Mary Webb's second novel, says Mr. John Buchan, who afterwards came to know the author personally, 'was published in the dark days of 1917. It was the first of Mary Webb's novels to come into my hands. I read it at a time when everything that concerned the soil of England seemed precious.' How precious it had become to Mary Webb herself we know already. Millions of 'creatures who could love so much,' in John Morley's phrase, were being thrust into an inferno of fury, millions of brave, loving men had 'gone to earth'; so that the novel may in some measure be regarded as symbolical, filled with the echo of an 'awful and piercing' voice, 'deep with unutterable horror' — the description is the author's at the end of her story —

'the voice of a soul driven mad by torture. . . . And at its awful reiteration the righteous men and the hunt ceased to be people of any class or time or creed, and became creatures swayed by one primeval passion, fear. They crouched and shuddered like beaten dogs as the terrible cry once more roused the shivering echoes: "Gone to earth! Gone to earth!" '

It is the book of one who had looked deep into life at all times, not only during the years 'when nights are dark and mornings dim.' The manifold problems of existence, inevitable, shattering, had brought pain to her eyes – pain that compelled her to give utterance to her troubled mind. The symbolism of *Gone to Earth* clearly reveals her attitude to life – a phrase which at this stage of her work is preferable to claiming it as a philosophy. She perceived two forces in life, good and evil, spiritual and material, the spiritual wholly good, depicting the character of God, the material always evil, and especially evil the more it is identified with the world as distinct from the earth. 'Oh filthy, heavy-handed, blear-eyed world,' cries Mary Webb, 'when will you wash and be clean?' Cruelty is, for her, the world's worst evil – all the rest arises out of cruelty. Contact with the world, with materialistic life, being a necessity of human existence, men and women and the animals that are linked together are bound to suffer. Spirituality, the non-materialistic, is only a small part of the common life: and if an individual is enlightened by more than the average spirituality he suffers abnormally, because of his contact with materialistic forces. The chief character in *Gone to Earth*, Hazel Woodus, is crushed altogether by these forces. In death alone she found refuge – she is 'gone to earth.' And Hazel, by the magic of the artist, thus becomes at one with all the martyred idealists of history, the persecuted who were stoned by the mob, or flung into the arena of wild beasts, or burned at the stake, or nailed to the Cross.

The world against which Hazel Woodus was pitted so ruthlessly is that of a handful of people almost in the same corner of the countryside where dwelt John Arden and his daughter Deborah, and Eli and Lily and Joe, in *The Golden Arrow*. Again we feel 'the Presences in the shadows on the hill' under which the tale of Hazel Woodus and her persecutors winds out its agonizing length. Again we feel that, as Mr. Buchan points out, 'the winds and seasons, day and night' and in this instance 'God's Little Mountain, the Callow, Hunter's Spinney, the house of Undern,' are as much alive in the drama as the men and women.

146

They take sides in the tragedy: those that the influence of materiality has left untouched are ranged with Hazel, those that have been tainted by evil are against her. She herself, a girl not yet woman, a child of nature, is bound to suffer, 'since she can never adjust herself to the strait orbit of human life.' She expresses in all she says and does a life of the spirit, like any child until it comes into contact with ordinary existence. Her pity for suffering creatures of the wild is not human, it is Christlike.

'"I canna bear this place," said Hazel; "it's so drodsome."

'"Awhile since, afore you were born, a cow fell down that there place, hundreds of feet."

'"Did they save her?"

'"Laws, no! She was all of a jelly."

'Hazel broke out with sudden passionate crying. "Oh, dunna, dunna!" she sobbed. So she did always at any mention of helpless suffering, flinging herself down in wild rebellion and abandonment so that epilepsy had been suspected. But it was not epilepsy. It was pity. She, in her inexpressive, childish way, shared with the love-martyr of Galilee the heartrending capacity for imaginative sympathy. In common with him and others of her kind, she was not only acquainted with grief, but reviled and rejected. In her schooldays boys brought maimed frogs and threw them into her lap, to watch, from a safe distance, her almost crazy grief and rage.'

Hazel is not wholly friendless in her brief isolated life, and we meet with that friend in the very opening pages, even before we encounter the girl herself:

'Between the larch boles and under the thickets of honeysuckle and blackberry came a tawny, silent form, wearing with the calm dignity of woodland creatures a beauty of eye and limb, a brilliance of tint, that few women could have worn without self-consciousness. Clear-eyed, lithe, it stood for a moment in the full sunlight – a year-old fox, round-headed and velvet-footed. Then it slid into the shadows. A shrill whistle came from the interior of the wood, and the fox bounded towards it.

' "Where you bin? You'm stray and lose yourself, certain sure!" said a girl's voice, chidingly motherly. "And if you'm alost, I'm

alost; so come you whome. The sun's under-
ing, and there's bones for supper!" '

The first picture that is presented to us of
Hazel and Foxy, standing together in the
lane above the cottage, is ominous. 'The red
light from the west stained Hazel's torn old
dress, her thin face, her eyes, till she seemed
to be dipped in blood. The fox, wistfulness in
her expression and the consciousness of coming
supper in her mind, gazed obediently where
her mistress gazed; and was touched with the
same fierce beauty.' Indeed, in the ensuing
comment we perceive that the author intends
the picture to be ominous. 'They stood there
fronting the crimson pools over the far hills,
two small sentient things facing destiny with
pathetic courage; they had, in the chill evening
on the lonely hill, a look of those pre-destined
to grief, almost an air of martyrdom.'
Two men enter into Hazel's young life, and
they are less her friends than this dumb creature of the woods. Both love her, but with the
love that means cruelty. There is Jack Reddin,
the callous sensualist, 'who never stays his
appetite'; master of Undern Hall, of the many
small-paned windows, that 'faced the north

sullenly,' 'a place of which the influence and magic were not good.' There is also Edward Marston, the minister, who strives for spiritual development, but is held back by his humanness, which includes a limitation of understanding.

Edward Marston lived at God's Little Mountain, where

'the chapel and minister's house were all in one – a long, low building of grey stone surrounded by the graveyard, where stones, flat, erect and askew, took the place of a flower garden. . . . Not the least of the mysteries of the place, and it was tense with mystery, was the Sunday congregation, which appeared to spring up miraculously from the rocks, woods and graves.'

Edward 'had always been naturally religious, taking on trust what he was taught: and he had an instinctive pleasure in clean and healthy things. But on winter nights at the mountain, when the tingling stars sprang in and out of their black ambush and frost cracked the tombstones; in summer, when lightning crackled in the woods and ripped along the hillside like a thousand devils, the need of a God grew ever more urgent.'

With Edward, whom the world has made

so stereotyped that the rebellious part of him is fascinated by the frail woodland girl, Hazel Woodus finds shelter. She does not escape the frowns of the other convention-ridden people, especially Edward's mother, whose attitude to the marriage of her son is that of somebody totally blind, yet in her blindness spiteful to one who had come from a cottage 'very low, one-storied, and roofed with red corrugated iron, little larger than a good pigsty'; and from a father, Abel Woodus, who played the harp and kept bees, and made the coffin whenever a villager died. Abel was outwardly drab, but his love of music touches him with poetry. So does his bee-lore:

'Whenever an order for a coffin came, Hazel went to tell the bees who was dead. Her father thought this unnecessary. It was only for folks that died in the house, he said. But he had himself told the bees when his wife died. He had gone out on that vivid June morning to his hives, and had stood watching the lines of bees fetching water, their shadows going and coming on the clean white boards. Then he had stooped and said with a curious confidential indifference: "Maray's jead." He had put his ear to the hive and listened to the deep, solemn murmur within; but it was the murmur of the future, and not of the past, the pre-occupation with life, not with death, that filled the pale galleries within.'

This passage has an illuminating predecessor in modern fiction. It is to be found in Walter Raymond's *Love and Quiet Life*, published forty years ago:

'The upstairs windows, small and square under the overhanging thatch, were as blank as death; and underneath, by the row of bee-butts, dimly visible through the dusk, crouched Granmer.

' "She's a-tellin the bees."

'The old woman passed from butt to butt, laying her lips close to the mouth of each.

' "The wold man's a-gone," she said. "The wold man's a-tookt to the last." '

V

What the poet Richard le Gallienne called the pathos of eternity sighs through these old-world country customs. The same pathos clings to all Hazel's little history. Between the crude materialism of Reddin, who pursues her and drags her from her refuge, and the blundering pseudo-spirituality of Marston, she is buffeted until the only way out is in merciful death; merciful, although when it comes to her it seems as cruel as life had been. Ostensibly Hazel sacrifices her life as she seeks to save 'Foxy' from the hounds – actually it is she whom they pursue until she is driven over the rocks of the quarry – the victim of man's cruelty and his love. Being human, she was sufficiently earth-bound to desire that love, but Marston, with mistaken motive, denies her: on the other hand Reddin refuses her spiritual love and refuses it far more grossly than Stephen Southernwood had denied it to Deborah Arden in *The Golden Arrow*.

Grouped about these three principal characters in *Gone to Earth* are a number of minor people, and there is more than one triumph of portraiture among them, notably Andrew Vessons, Reddin's servant, who reminds us of Shakespeare's gravediggers in his philosophizing while he is at work. He takes as direct a part in the actual story as any. When Hazel leaves Edward Marston after some months of marriage and is enticed back to Undern Hall by Reddin, she arouses anew the jealousy and anger of Vessons. In his clumsy desperation he seeks to drive her away from Undern, and so arranges that Reddin's earlier mistress, Sally, by whom he has had several children, shall come into the house and confront Hazel. The ensuing scene is excellent in its irony:

'. . . Vessons set out for Sally's, anxious that she should be quick. But Sally would not hurry. It was washing-day, and she also insisted on making all the children very smart, unaware that their extreme ugliness was her strength. It was not until three o'clock that she arrived at the front door, baby in arms, the four children, heavily expectant, at her heels, and Vessons stage-managing in the background. . . .

'"Who be you?" she (Hazel) asked in a frightened voice as they eyed her.

'"I'm Sally Haggard and these be my children." She surveyed them proudly. "D'you notice that they favour anyone?"

'Hazel looked at them timidly.

'"They favour you," she said.

'"Not Mr. Reddin?"

'"Mr. Reddin?"

'"Ah. They'd ought to. They'm his'n."

' "His'n?"

' "Yes, parrot."

' "Be you the 'ooman as Martha said Jack lived along of?"

' "He did live along of me."

' "Why then, you'd ought to be Mrs. Reddin, and wear this gownd, and live at Undern," said Hazel.

' "Eh?" Sally was astonished.

' "And he said there wunna any other but me."

'Sally laughed.

' "You believed that lie? You little softie!"

'Hazel looked at the children.

' "Be they *all* his'n?" she said.

' "Every man-jack of 'em, and not so much as a thank you for me!"

'The children were ranged near their mother — on high chairs. They gaped at Hazel, sullen and critical. An irrepressible question broke from Hazel.

' "What for did you have 'em?"

'Sally stared.

' "What for?" she repeated. "Surely to goodness, girl, you're not so innicent-like as that?"

' "I ain't ever going to have any," Hazel went on with great firmness, as she eyed the children.

155

' "God above!" muttered Sally. 'He's fooled her worse'n me!"

' "Come and look at the baby, my dear," she said in a voice astonishingly soft. She looked at Hazel keenly. "Dunna you know?" she asked.

' "What?"

' "As you're going to have a baby?" '

The whole book glitters with dark-fired gems of drama as clean-cut and impressive as that passage. Everywhere the technical advance on *The Golden Arrow* is manifest; supremely, of course, in the way Mary Webb holds our sympathy for Hazel, who might in less astute care have been tiresome; but also in such scenes as that of the wedding, of the clashes between Hazel and her aunt, and Hazel and her mother-in-law. Rich comedy is here to soften a tragedy that stabs at the reader fiercely. Perhaps Mary Webb's one failure in the book is where she allows the search for Hazel by Reddin across the countryside in the early chapters to approach the grotesque.

The style is always distinguished, and the streaks of poetry become more and more frequent as the story proceeds. The beauty of nature is emphasized everywhere – the beauty of woodland and sky, cloud, rain, wind, leaf, bird and beast. Everything fits the setting, and the author's chief triumph lies in the fact that never does the questioning of a thinking, vital and progressive mind seem an intrusion. God, truth, love, happiness, religion: all are discussed in a manner that fits naturally into the story, as when Hazel says in explanation of the wrong Reddin had done her:

' "Maybe you were druv to it."
' "Who by?" he asked, with an attempt at flippancy.
'Hazel's eyes were dark and hunted. "Summat strong and drodsome, as drives us all," she said.
'She had a vision of all the world racing madly round and round, like the exhausted and terrified horse Reddin had that morning lunged. But what power it was that stood in the centre, breaking without an effort the spirit of the mad, fleeing, tethered creature, she could not tell.'

And even the direct philosophical utterance, that which holds up the narrative for the moment, is a part of the splendidly complete novel. The passage describes how 'all through the night, murmurous with little rivulets of snow-water, the gurgling of full troughing, and the patter of rain on the iron roof of the house, and the miniature roofs of the beehives,' Hazel heard over and over again some words she had listened to, that had prophesied her fate. And then:

'In her frightened dreams she reached out to something that she felt must be beyond the pleasant sound of falling water, so small and transitory; beyond the drip and patter of human destinies — something vast, solitary, and silent. How should she find that which none had ever named or known. Men only stammer of it in such words as Eternity, Fate, God. All the out-cries of all creatures, living and dying, sink in its depth as in an unsounded ocean.

'Whether this listening silence, incurious, yet hearing all, is benignant or malevolent, who can say? The wistful dreams of men haunt this theme for ever: the creeds of men are so many keys that do not fit the lock. We ponder it in our hearts, and some find peace, and some find terror. The silence presses upon us ever more heavily until Death comes with his cajoling voice and promises us the key. Then we run after him into the stillness, and are heard no more.'

CHAPTER SIX

The Cottage on a Hill – and '*The House in Dormer Forest*'

I

SO happy was Mary Webb on her native soil, so unhappy elsewhere, that it would be hard to find a fitter description of her than that of 'The Shropshire Lass,' by Mr. G. K. Chesterton, in his foreword to a volume in the edition of the novels collected since her death. Absence from the only place she ever thought of as home oppressed her more and more acutely as the war-years drifted by. During her moods of what she described in a poem as the old home-sickness vast and dumb, she wrote 'The Land Within.' Here she disavows the actuality, except in her own deluded mind, of the distant life for which she yearned so passionately. 'The Land Within' makes its appeal to the understanding and sympathy of those who, after many years, have returned to the old corner of earth with which their original memories are associated; and there and then, in the first moving moment of return, have perceived that however contented and even happy they seemed to be in exile they were missing something all the time. Others who have never been enlightened at first-hand as to the deep-rootedness of our early affections, may regard as strained and fantastic, or as concerned merely with the reflection of forests and stars in lake-waters, the poet's questionings, and her answer: —

'Was there a sound of leaves here once, and streams
    Gurgling on pebbles? (In dreams, my soul! in dreams.)
Galleons of golden lilies then could ride
Safely, though coot and moorhen stirred the tide,
Swimming with all their young, and loud sweet cries
Fell from the mountains where the curlew haunted
Green mossy cwms, sun-drenched and thrice enchanted;
And somewhere in the lakes confused reflections,
Remote and fair as childhood's recollections,
Smothered in wavering lilac leaves, and blurred
With bloom, the shadow of a gable stirred

160

With every tide, and a twisted chimney
    flowered
In pale blue smoke, that in the water towered
Downward. And through those deeps, pillared
    and aisled,
Came a brown woodman, and a boy who
    smiled,
Running towards the shifting wicket-gate,
And waved an under-water hand, to spy
One leaning from the casement – that was I.

'Where was the cottage with its lilac trees,
Its windows wide, its garden drowsed with
    bees?
Where stood the echoing glade whence the
    faggot came
To turn the evening hours to one warm flame?
And that brown woodman, where and whence
    was he –
That woodman with the eyes that dazzled me
Far more than rosy fire or golden gleams
Of April? O, in dreams, my soul! in dreams.'

    The only certain cure for dreams that sap the
dreamer's vitality is to bring that 'land within'
back to outward reality, thus making the
'sound of leaves,' the 'green mossy cwms, sun-
drenched,' the cottage with its lilac trees, the

'echoing glade,' more than memories. Therefore Mr. Webb, feeling it imperative to secure a professional appointment in the vicinity of Shrewsbury so that they could live there uninterruptedly, sought and obtained one at The Priory School in September, 1916. A more convenient dwelling-place than Rose Cottage or The Nills Farm at Pontesbury was also decided upon, and the Webbs turned to Lyth Hill, which had always been an object of Mary Webb's thoughts. In her young womanhood at Meole Brace she was lured to its uplands with pencil and writing-pad, day after day, in the early morning. Later on, she tramped from Pontesbury to Shrewsbury market, and went sometimes by way of the hill, although it took her miles from the track of the crow's flight.

At first they lived in furnished rooms at one of the houses near the summit; but eventually, 'by juggling that now seems marvellous to me,' Mr. Webb recalls, 'we raised the money to build a place of our own.' With a hundred pounds, advanced by Mary Webb's mother, they purchased a field delightfully untamed, a rough-and-tumble stretch of grass, stones and bracken; and then they persuaded the bank to lend a further £250 on mortgage – also a marvellous feat, especially as it was done in war-time. With this money and the aid of a friendly builder, 'Spring Cottage' came into being: a bungalow erected according to Mary Webb's own plans, which plans gave her such enthusiasm that she sent copies of the drawing to her friends.

The bungalow was a modest place, one-storied, built of plain red brick, and possessing only two rooms and a scullery. At the doorway you look straight across to Caer Caradoc, the Long Mynd, the Devil's Chair, and – what is more important to note at this stage – somewhere in the blue mists, beyond the cornfields that in April are miraculously smouldering with green, in August miraculously ablaze with gold, Dormer Old House.

II

Very different from Spring Cottage, modern, flimsy by contrast, was the dwelling-place which immediately the Webbs had settled on Lyth Hill early in 1917, was to become the principal character in her third novel, *The House in Dormer Forest*.

'From these heights, in fine weather, the house and its gardens lay open to the view, small

163

but clear, beside the white thread that was Dormer Brook. The place had been patched and enlarged by successive generations, very much as man's ideas are altered, the result in both cases being the same – a mansion to the majority, a prison to the few. On clear evenings when the westering sun struck up the valley and set the windows on fire, one could see the centuries in the house, like ferns in a fossil.'

Such is the dwelling-place of sinister influence which is presented in the opening chapter of the novel with similar vividness to that of Thomas Hardy's description of the heath in *The Return of the Native* – Egdon,

'the place full of a watchful intentness now; for when other things sank brooding to sleep the heath appeared slowly to awake and listen. Every night its Titanic form seemed to await something: but it had waited thus unmoved, during so many centuries, through the crisis of so many things, that it could only be imagined to await one last crisis – the final overthrow.'

Mary Webb adopted the method of Hardy and Eden Phillpotts in opening the story of her house at the edge of the forest of Dormer, for no human character appears on the scene until the second chapter. That the house itself was entitled to this immediate importance may be indicated in another way. Her first title for the novel was 'The House of Peril.' She discarded it for *The House in Dormer Forest* because, to her disappointment, she learnt that in a contemporary play on the London stage she had been forestalled. She had her consolation, however: the later title, she came to realize, was less melodramatic, more worthy of the work itself.

Her earlier novels had been written quickly, as we have seen: but she worked only slowly at this book, and occasionally it would seem as though her artistic confidence deserted her, for some of the ideas are repetitions of those in her earlier novels. Apart from the main theme of the old, worn-out country house that has a perilous influence on its inhabitants, and in which Dormer House resembles the Undern Hall of *Gone to Earth*, we have again the theory that fresh peasant blood has the power to restore the effete stock of the 'quality,' as in the case of Hazel and Reddin, of the same novel.

Moreover, Dormer House is burnt down: so was the cottage in *The Golden Arrow*. The symbolism in each instance is similar. When the spirit of life has vanished out of anything the material shell is of no account, and is fit only to be destroyed.

But it would be wrong to emphasize these parallels without adding that in the majority of them *The House in Dormer Forest* shows a definite advancement, as though the author had carried each parallel a step further in spiritual development, even though the physical state may have remained as it was. Admittedly Ruby Darke, 'a tall plump pretty girl of eighteen' who, at the beginning of the human part of the story has been discovered 'sprawling across the table,' is mainly a replica of Lily Huntbatch in *The Golden Arrow*, who 'took stock of Deborah jealously; detested her for having blue ribbon and a normal father; and put an arm round her waist to disguise the fact and to see if Deborah had made her waist smaller by tight-lacing.' But Enoch in *The House in Dormer Forest* is a richer portrait of the father who was John Arden in that earlier novel — the origin of the combined names 'Enoch Arden' is elsewhere. 'Enoch was never quite at his ease in Dormer. He liked to be out on the huge purple hills under the towering sky, where the curlews cried out strange news to him in passing, and the little brown doves murmured of a hidden country, a secret land, more limited than those of man, yet miraculous. . . .' A fragment of his talk amply reveals him:

' "Enoch," said Jasper, "are we astray, or are they?"

' "Oh, if it's to be in good sadness, Master Jasper, I canna say fairer than — 'I dunna know.' May 'appen we'm all strays. Maybe we'll ne'er find out till Time's gone by." '

Late in the book there is an expression of astonishment 'that Enoch, of all people, should develop these murderous tendencies!'

Amber Darke, another of Mary Webb's beautiful heroines, is Deborah Arden again, but less crude, more aware of life and herself — and incidentally the author's self-portrait in her young womanhood —

'her hair was of an indeterminate brown, her complexion was ruined by ill-health, due to the perpetual chafing of the wistful mind longing for things not in Dormer. . . .

'In many a poor home she had seen a light that never shone at Dormer: seen the chalice lifted in whose mingled wine is agony and ecstasy: heard those bells pealing out into the rainy, windy night of time which swing only in the mysterious belfries of the human heart. Sometimes when she came late through the village she would see an oblong of crocus light that seemed to come not only from the cheap lamp and the carefully tended fire.'

But wholly new figures are to be added to Mary Webb's gallery out of *The House in Dormer Forest*. Especially is there the grandmother, oracle of the family, Mrs. Velindre, with her strong Scriptural relish. If someone were recommended to join the army she would chime in with 'Fight the good fight!' Her laugh was 'like the sound of the winter wind in the old ivy of Dormer, like the sigh of freezing water.' And she inherited a rigid code of conduct that, if it could not always be squared with her religion, led to a grotesque compromise.

' "I mind," said grandmother, "how my Aunt Deborah brought me here to buy a white gown to be bishoped in. I was but eleven. The Bishop didn't come often, and you had to get rid of Sattan when you could. I hid an applecob in my pocket (Sattan being in me at the time), and the grease showed. Aunt Deborah said: 'Bishoped you *may* be. That's the will of the Lord. Birched you *shall* be. That's mine.' " '

The tragedy of *The House in Dormer Forest* is that of outworn creeds and customs stifling aspiration, strangling the soul. There is but one true way of life – to venture upon changes fearlessly, to cast aside all that hinders or threatens to make existence stereotyped. The family who live at Dormer are eight in number: Mrs. Velindre, the matriarchal grandmother, her daughter Rachel Darke, wife of Solomon Darke, who is the head of the house, and mother of two sons, Peter and Jasper, and of two daughters, Ruby and Amber; there is also Catherine Velindre, a distant relation who lives with them as a paying guest, and calls Mr. and Mrs. Darke 'uncle' and 'aunt' as terms of respect. Minor characters are Enoch, the hired man, and Sarah, the servant, a creature of earth, racy in speech and performance, unromantic and unimaginative, uncannily gifted with the power to discern concealed motives, expressing herself about them with virile aptness: a serving-woman, indeed, who at times seems to be the whole life and support of the household. Sarah is assisted by Mrs. Gosling and Marigold Gosling, her daughter, a young servant prettier in her looks

169

than in her speech, notably when she reckoned that 'Master Peter'll be King o' the midden' if it comes to fists!'

The daily life of Dormer House, gloomy, tradition-ravaged, is presented in its manifold aspects, and the manner in which these diverse temperaments act and react on each other is meticulously described. The impulses, instincts, motives, desires, and hopes are analysed in each separate personality and then in the group. There is Amber, upon whose modest, grateful, and generous nature the influence of the house is continually pressing:

'The house lay dumb under the night. To Amber it seemed that its quiet had the quality of the spider's, mutely awaiting the faintly vocal fly. . . . She sprang up with a defensive feeling, and went into the hall. As she pulled open the heavy door, the voice of the stream, swollen by the autumn rains, smote upon her suddenly, full of sad foreboding. It was deepened by the low, sonorous sound of the Four Waters, half a mile away — a monotonous and bee-like note that seemed to have been struck before the beginning of time. Dormer, in its cup at the bases of the hills, was always full of damp air and the sound of water. Besieged by this grievous music – and what is there in nature sadder than the lament of falling water? – she felt as if she had opened the door not to the night and the stream, but on to a future full of doubt and dread, veiled in mist.'

But – and in this passage is revealed one of Mary Webb's motives for writing the novel (if we dare attribute motives to a novelist) –

'Amber thought of June mornings when polished birds with flaming yellow bills made large tracks in the dew-white grass. She thought of the subtle changes of the seasons, breathlessly fair, not one to be spared. She remembered dawns that bloomed like a hedge of roses above the amethyst hills, and the bank of white violets, which had never missed her yet in April. These things were her home, not Dormer.'

Amber eventually triumphs over that sinister environment, just as Enoch, the hired man, triumphs in his less sensitive fashion, for he too has 'the love of nature that is a passion for those in whom it once lodges.' Not so Catherine, however, diametrically opposite as she is in character, cold, hard, selfish, ungenerous, cruel, wanton; or Ruby, the shallow and flippant one, barren of finer understanding. A generation older than these, and therefore personages on whom the influence of Dormer has become heavily marked, are Mrs. Darke, the mother, hard as Ruby, loveless and unloving, whose repressions find outlet in cruelty and callousness – strongly resembling Eli Huntbatch in *The Golden Arrow*; and Solomon Darke, shadowy, indifferent to all except his dogs. Peter also is repressed, but vaguely rebellious in a way that fades into easy-going conduct, mundane emotions, and generally in taking life 'as it comes.' His brother, Jasper, is nearer to Amber in his desires and aspirations, but failing in his search for God he throws up his training for the Church and incurs the wrath of all Dormer.

Jasper loves Catherine Velindre, whose religious words and looks render her acceptable to another in the house, his brother Peter, the cynic, 'not because they were real, but because she looked and spoke with the eyes and lips of a courtesan.' When Jasper disappoints the family by withdrawing from his theological studies and is obliged to become a farm-hand, it is Dormer House that dictates to Catherine what her attitude shall be. She refuses to marry Jasper while he is an infidel. Peter, however, has in the meanwhile turned to the housemaid Marigold, who, to the confusion of the Dormer traditions, acts, with her 'may-tree freshness, her rose and gold and white,' as outlet for the complications of Peter's emotional life, that will not be thwarted by his cynicism.

Ruby is wedded to a clergyman, but the curse of the house is on her also, and her greedy ambition for white satin and a veil proves, when fulfilled, to be no compensation for the bitterness of loveless marriage. On the other hand, when Michael Hallowes comes with love to Amber, she responds with a sweetness and purity of instinct that have remained untainted.

Situation rather than movement is presented in *The House in Dormer Forest*. Action is summed up in a walk, a ride, a meal, a quarrel, a wedding. But the circumstances themselves keep the story in constant flow.

'A crowd of people shut up together in one house, one creed, one strait view of life, must eventually wear each other out. Good nature is ground down by constant friction. Hatred leaps out like sparks from flint and iron. Society thinks that mistakes are made and crimes committed through the human soul being too much itself, going its own way. But crimes really happen through the soul being too little itself, striving to conform, or being crushed into conformity.'

That the house in Dormer Forest is burnt to the ground in the last chapter – by the old grandmother, appropriately! – is an end with symbolism as well as reality. The release for all who have been its prisoners is spiritual and material.

'Enoch carried grandmother downstairs, looking, in his large embrace, like a Red Indian's doll. Her dark, pleased, slightly malicious face was lit by the red light as they passed through the danger zone.

' "I did it! I did it!" she cried.

' "Most a pity if you did, mum, as you can boast of it," said Sarah. But grandmother only laughed her rustling laugh. Enoch set her down in the church porch, where she huddled like a winter bird, only her eyes alive, with their old look as of unknown creatures stalking in their depths. She surveyed the blazing house with complaisance. Then she said:

' "A burnt offering to the Lord. Hannah Velindre shall be called blessed. Dormer's falling!" '

174

Not that the household of the Darkes was unanimous in regarding the burning of Dormer House as a release, nor that old Hannah Velindre was regarded by them as 'blessed.' Mrs. Darke, Rachel,

'was stunned as a long-caged animal is at the sight of open doors. She would never hear the solemn, deathly night-sounds of Dormer again: never pace her grey bedroom. Grandmother had destroyed it all. Here she was, shivering, outcast, lonely, the house she trusted in dissolved, the restrictions that upheld her removed. She had lived according to the ghostly will of the house until her faint desire for freedom and development had died. Freedom was a dream; when it had gone, she slept the better. And now, here she was, with nothing between her and the stars. . . .'

But Rachel's resolve to punish that incendiary old lady was thwarted, for —

'She nudged her mother. "Wake up," she said. Grandmother fell in a stiff heap at her feet. She lay there like a broken idol that no man remembers. She was never to go tapping round with her stick again. It is ill to look upon the old gods in their last downfall. With a vertiginous horror, Rachel knew that her mother was dead. Brown, wrinkled, hard, the old face lay, smiling in the secure knowledge that Hannah Velindre was to be called blessed.'

IV

Mary Webb wrote *The House in Dormer Forest* with the consciousness that she now possessed the 'lovely impossible things I long for,' that she had specified in a letter to a friend: 'to live on Lyth Hill, and to live in a house of my own.' But more and more the world-tragedy distracted her, and the novel suggests a conflict of faith and disillusionment, in which first one and then the other is uppermost.

It was begun as a tragedy. The drowning of Jasper was intended to form the climax to the story. But before she had completed the first half, a strong sense of the grotesque and ironical assailed her, and eventually she resolved to bring the drowned man back to life. Much of the faultiness and lack of inevitability in the plot is explained by this. Indeed there are times when Mary Webb's imaginative power seems to have been displaced by intellectual theorising. Perhaps, however, this ought not to be regretted over-much, for the maturity of a rich mind is thereby vouchsafed to us. She speaks of idealism, of spirit and matter, of mysticism, humanitarianism, laughter, social freedom, love, marriage, nationalism, the herd and the individual, time and space, and even the Jews: 'She (Mrs. Velindre) persisted in regarding the Jews not as one of the finest nations the world has seen, but as people requiring a missionary.' . . .

Of the herd and the individual: 'She had for so many years been trying to be like other people, that she was now like nothing in heaven or earth. For the more a soul conforms to the sanity of others, the more does it become insane. By continually doing violence to its own laws, it finally loses the power of governing itself.'

And, of time and space in relation to the same herd, the same individual: 'Where man is massed, there he seems doomed to live by rule and by time. Those who dare to be themselves are not so bounded. For the lover time is changeable; a moment of absence wears on him like a year, and a year with the beloved is gone like a falling star.'

Of the idealist she says that 'if the world lets him alone he keeps his childhood until he dies. He only loses it if some great emotional tempest ravages his being to the depths.' Explaining why the eyes of those who grow near to the spiritual ideal may be 'dull and sad,' she writes that

'this is often so with minds of peculiar strength or tenderness. The world lays such heavy burdens on them that something must break. The soul is impregnable, so the body breaks. The people whose eyes are clear pools are usually those who, being completely vacant in soul, put all their vitality into physical well-being and have a good digestion.'

She expresses her muteness at the thought of religion in this passage better than elsewhere:

'Alas, alas for us who in these latter days find the wan hills all silent and deserted, with none to beckon us to certain peace, with no noise of angels in the silver clouds. Yet when the solemn wind begins to move along the mountains, walking in the heavy trees; when every dewy leaf has a gleam of recognition for the wet-eyed stars, does there not come upon us in a sweetness greater than the fragrance of flowers, a desire, passionate and vague, for a beauty that is not less real because its revelations are subtle and its essence beyond the reach of the senses?'

Occasionally her philosophic mood is allowed

in this novel to intrude upon her artistry. When Jasper goes to the water so that he may end his troubles there, he cannot help being unduly the nature-lover:

'As he went, he did not think of Catherine, with her predatory purity; nor of Dormer, with its vault-like air; nor of his love, trampled and dead. He thought of watergreen, saffron, blue, brown, white, every colour. His mind became for those moments the mind of a water-creature. He dreamed the dreams of the long-rooted lily, the darting trout, the caddis, moving on its secret enterprises, clad in its brook-finery of little stones and nestling in the sand. The coot and the vole, the water scorpion, and the bull-head that hides under the stones – those were his intimates. He knew them in a flash of time – their desires, their passion. They lived for the silver water; in the water they died. He also was impassioned for water – since it gave a velvet-soft wound, opened a green, easy corridor down into death.

'Yes! that was where he would go, down where the water-buttercup rooted, and the rosy-budded milfoil swayed, and that strange sorcery-breathing bloom, the buckbean, planted its feet in the mud. Peace was there – golden peace, where the great clumps of tansy and figwort made all day long a brown and yellow blur upon the sheet of steel; dark blue and silver peace, where a rift of night sky slashed the grey current and held far within it the sad, clear eye of a star; black, stirless peace, where a yew tree laid its great bulk upon the pale water, like a weary giant on his bed.'

But this does not detract from the poignancy of the delayed climax:

'He stood beneath the yew tree that was shaped like a monkey, and let his eyes dwell on the murmuring flood, while he tried, with youth's bepuzzled frown, to visualize Dormer without himself in it. There they would all be, busy, absorbed in outward observance, and Catherine would buy a becoming black dress. Suddenly he realized that, instead of his personality being fainter because of his death, it would for the first time be really ponderable.

'He laughed at that – the wild laugh of a soul unmoored by some great shock from the safe and homely things of life.

'Then he heard Sarah, back in the garden, calling: "Eenoch!"

'It brought the world in, and the fear of being afraid, of being once more tied down to the daily life he hated.

'The water closed over him with a soft, assenting lisp.'

The perfect blend of nature-philosophy and art is to be found in the scene of the plighting of Michael and Amber:

'She looked up at last and found his eyes on her. With a catch of the breath she said:

' "Of course, Michael. We must go – away."

'Her voice trembled into lostness.

'Michael sighed. The tension had been almost unbearable.

' "You love me enough to be willing to go?"

' "I have said so. You are stern to-night."

' "You're a very beautiful woman, Amber. And if we go, I'll make it up to you."

'He spoke with self-reliance, having enough insight to know that the man a woman loves can make up to her for anything on earth.

' "What fairing shall I buy you, out in the world, Amber?"

' "Nothing."

' "Is there nothing that will repay you – the delights of big cities? Finding yourself?"

' "No."

'He was silent. Around them the forest took up its night-spinning of multitudinous little sounds. Sigh and rustle and soft footfall, ruffled feather, falling of early seed vessels, and that dream of a sound, the stealing of dew on to every leaf and blade and mossy bed — all blending in a vague half-music.

'Michael brooded on the leafy layers below them, on the glow-worm lights which were all of the world that he could see. While she groped intuitively, he saw the situation starkly and clearly. The temptation to let this moment pass, to let the crisis remain unspoken, to let their lives go on with the important things tacit, unexpressed, took hold of him fiercely. But he never treated life in this way. He took a little medallion out of his pocket, and striking a match on his boot, held it before her.

' "That?" he asked.

' "Yes, Michael."

' "In poverty and discomfort? In crude places beyond the sea? In the squalor of big cities?"

' "You make it all very hard, Michael."

' "Life is hard."

' "Well, then, yes."

' "Risking death?"

' "Michael, Michael! Let me be happy to-night! Let me!"

' "Risking death?" His voice was harsh. "Do you think I shall let you say 'yes, yes!' in your eager way, without first making you realize?"

' "There are some things in life that cannot be bought except at that risk, Michael. They are worth it."

'Her voice sank in the purple silence. The little medallion of the Madonna and Child slipped from her lap.

' "Don't think I care about it at all, Amber."

' "No?"

' "I'd just as soon – not."

' "What a dreadful lie, Michael!"

'He looked up with the shyly guilty air of a small delinquent. She loved that look.

' "And so brazen!" she added, stroking his hair. Michael knelt on the moss with his arms about her. He was silent, but the forest, with a deep and solemn murmur, spoke his heart.'

That is only one of several exquisite love-scenes in Mary Webb's novels. It is the loveli-est scene in *The House in Dormer Forest*, and if the complaint be made that it hardly befits the sombreness which precedes it, the answer is to be found in Shakespeare's *The Merchant of Venice*, with its equally incongruous and lovely end to sombreness. Let us accept it as a footnote to a work that cannot be treated only as a novel.

CHAPTER SEVEN

Prelude to 'Precious Bane'

I

THE Great War had ended, and the world of books and readers was reverting to a more normal course by the time *The House in Dormer Forest* appeared. No longer was it possible for a work of merit to be ignored if it failed to concern itself either directly or by implication with the war. Indeed, there were signs that many people wished to have their thoughts wholly distracted.

Not that the London publishers had been without encouragement for meritorious writing even while the unprecedented difficulties which confronted them during the years of upheaval threatened their worst. Three books by Mary Webb herself, unknown author that she was, had been accepted and published. Doubtless the publishers' interest in her was strengthened by the tribute which Miss Rebecca West paid to her second novel in a symposium of the year's reading, contributed to a newspaper at the close of 1917. *Gone to Earth*, declared Miss West with characteristic fervour and fearlessness,

185

was the novel of the year, and its author 'a genius.'

So gratified by this was Mary Webb that she wrote immediately to Miss West, and her letter of thanks was the beginning of a correspondence which led to their personal association when, four years later, Mr. and Mrs. Webb went to live in London. Indeed, it was partly because of the prospect of meeting Miss West and one or two other discerning critics who had praised her work, and shown deep interest in it, that Shropshire was temporarily deserted. Until then Mary Webb treasured her correspondence with these unseen friends in a way that could not have been more humble and grateful were she a beginner. She sought relief from her disappointment at the lack of public appreciation of her novels by reading to those around her such passages in the letters she received from well-known authors that she could exclaim: '*They* think something of me!'

That the publishers regarded Mary Webb as a novelist of great potentialities is shown in their attitude to the manuscript of *The House in Dormer Forest*. The firm of Constable had issued *The Golden Arrow* and *Gone to Earth*.

But several other firms, including Hodder & Stoughton, in London, and Doubleday in New York, entered into competition for her third novel, which was eventually secured by Hutchinson & Company in England and George H. Doran in the U.S.A. The amounts which these publishers paid on account of 'advance royalties' will surprise anyone who has been inclined to exaggerate the statement made publicly after her death by the Right Hon. Stanley Baldwin that Mary Webb was 'an author who had not attained sufficient recognition.' 'Sufficient recognition' is a relative term, and the facts are that her new English publishers made a preliminary payment of £200 for *The House in Dormer Forest* and assured her a similar advance on her next novel; also the firm who proceeded to publish her books in America advanced £300 for *The House in Dormer Forest* and agreed to pay £300 for its successor. In order to make clear the significance of these amounts in relation to a novelist not yet 'established,' it may be explained that an advanced royalty of several hundred pounds on a single book is several times as large as the figure usually paid in similar circumstances before publication.

Mary Webb's fourth novel was *Seven for a Secret*. Mr. Robert Lynd has written: 'I do not suppose that many of the admirers of the work of Mary Webb – and they were a larger multitude during her lifetime than is generally realized – if asked to express an opinion as to which is the best of her books would name *Seven for a Secret*.' But although portions of this novel will lead the independent student to conclude that it had been written either when she was a relatively immature beginner or during a period of lowered creative vitality, he will at least grant that it was an admirable prelude to her masterpiece, *Precious Bane*.

The contemporary facts of Mary Webb's life support the theory that her creative vitality was not at its highest. Her medical adviser, indeed, had urged Mr. Webb to 'get her away for a change – to London preferably'; whereupon Mr. Webb secured a teaching-post at a school in North-west London, and in January, 1921, soon after the publication of *The House in Dormer Forest*, they closed the bungalow on Lyth Hill and transferred themselves to a furnished flat in Adelaide Road,

Hampstead. There they stayed for four months, and again we may turn to her verse for evidence of how the change, a drastic one, affected her sensitive nature. 'On Receiving a Box of Spring Flowers in London' suggests that in the tremendous hurly-burly of city traffic and smoky streets and mansion flats and unending speed and restlessness it was difficult even for her to believe that far-off Shropshire still existed, with its diametrically opposite kind of 'busy life':

'So the old, dear freemasonry goes on,
    The busy life, the laughter-under-sod,
The leafy hosts with spear and gonfalon
    Guarding the earthy mysteries of God.'

'I did not think the violets came so soon,' she continues, 'yet here are five, and all my room is sweet.' In 'Freedom' she utters a sigh of yearning:

'. . . Let us away, out of the murky day
Of sullen towns, into the silver noise
Of woods where every bird has found her way
Sunward, and every leaf has found a voice.'

She made her declaration about Nature's common happenings as though she sought to reassure herself that the buds and the leaves were still stirring in response to a cleaner, an unsullied Spring. . . . 'To a Blackbird Singing in London' suggests disillusionment with her new surroundings:

'Sing on, dear bird! Bring the old rapturous
        pain,
In this great town, where I no welcome find . . .'

Had Mary Webb been the only poet to give utterance to her thoughts in exile, these verses might be treated as merely the extravagances of an abnormal state of mind. Instead, like those of the major poets who, Nature-loving, were also city-pent, they are natural. And was it not inevitable that Mary Webb, with her earnestness and sincerity, her acute and ever-increasing sensitiveness concerning the physical effect of ill-health, should write as scornfully as she does in another poem, 'Safe,' about 'the endless talk, the critical, shy stare,' and should plead for escape —

'Safe from the world's long importunity —
 The endless talk, the critical, shy stare,
 The trifling social days — and unaware
 Of all the bitter thoughts they have of me,

Low in the grass, deep in the daisies,
I shall sleep sound, safe from their blames
and praises.'

III

'Transplanting to London,' Mary Webb's
husband has said, looking back, 'was not good
for her.'

Straitened circumstances, partly explained
by her inability to cope with the high cost of
living during those early post-war years, partly
by the decline in monetary value of the marriage
settlement made by her mother: an ominous if
slight recurrence of her old depressing malady:
disappointment with London, and above all,
with London literary life – these effected such
a revulsion in her that when Mr. and Mrs.
Webb returned to Lyth Hill for the Easter
vacation she resolved to remain there and concentrate on the novel she had begun tentatively
at Hampstead. For a brief while after Mr.
Webb resumed his teaching duties at Golder's
Green, Spring Cottage was her refuge. Mr.
Webb joined her there each week-end; but she
became lonely; and soon she was accompanying him back to London. And now they had a

place of their own, a tiny four-roomed cottage – incredibly tiny, spanning no more across it than twice the width of the front door – at 5 The Grove, in the older Hampstead, near the Underground Railway Station. It is hidden away in the quaint, Cranford-like corner that you pass almost without noticing as you climb the hill to the open heath. And here she determined to make the best of her transplanting. She asked editors for journalistic work, and wrote book reviews for the *Spectator* and the *Bookman*, in the latter journal concluding her article always with an unusual form of signature – 'Mary Webb (Mrs. H. B. L. Webb).' The editor, the late St. John Adcock, observed that she devoted as much care to this bread-and-butter writing as she did to her novels. Some of her short stories were published by Austin Harrison, editor of the *English Review*, whose courageous championship of unknown authors was not sufficiently acknowledged during his life nor has it been since his death. Also he introduced her to the P.E.N. Club of writers and editors, and supported her application for membership. There and at the meetings of the Bookman Circle and the To-morrow Club she met the majority of her contemporaries, especially rejoicing in the acquaintance of Mr. Walter de la Mare, to whose unique mind she was greatly attracted, and who delighted her by inviting her out to his Sunday afternoons at Anerley, and asking for permission to include three of her poems in his new anthology, *Come Hither*; of Mr. Stephen Graham ('it was a great evening,' she wrote in a letter about a P.E.N. Club dinner, 'for I sat next to Stephen Graham'); and of Miss Evelyn Underhill, whom she met as a fellow-guest at a gathering held by Miss May Sinclair at her club. One who admired her work was associated with a newspaper, and when he printed some of Mary Webb's verses, giving her the nominal but welcome remuneration of half a guinea each, she was quickly disillusioned as to the worldly appreciation of poetry. For her friend was asked by his editor: 'Why do you spend 10s. 6d. on a contribution by a living poet when you could get Wordsworth for nothing?'

IV

We catch personal glimpses of Mary Webb during those early years in London. At times she liked to be where 'the celebrities of a day, the noisy self-advertising boomsters,' were gathered together. From one standpoint she may be said to have worshipped success, though now and then in her books she scoffs at it, as when she says: 'In the world of art and literature the artist must elbow and push. . . . If he did not often stop his honeyed utterance to shout his wares he would not be heard at all.'

She was 'avid of excitement, experience, new sensations,' we have been told by the late Edwin Pugh.

'She had the curiosity of a cat. She wanted to know all about everything. She wanted to know London, and particularly the London slums. I told her that all I could show her would begin by disgusting and end by boring her; that no one ever had or ever would know London; that it would take her a lifetime even to get an inkling into its intimate secrets and mysteries; and that in any case she must live among Cockneys as one of themselves before she got to know even as much or as little as I knew about London, and its teeming millions; that London was a world in embryo, as foreign and remote from the most assiduous observer as her own countryside and people would be to me. She understood that, and never again broached the subject. . . .'

Mr. Pugh preserved a charming pen-picture of her in his description of their visit to the first performance of Mr. Caradoc Evans's play *Taffy* at a West-end theatre. She sat 'so enrapt, enthralled,' throughout the performance that her more sophisticated companion 'doubted if she had ever seen a properly staged play before, certainly not from the stalls. And yet she would have a cup of tea and a slice of cake when the refreshment-trays came round, and she could nibble chocolates all the time.' It was not difficult for her companion to imagine that she was living in her childhood once more, and that any jolly event was to her a kind of school-treat from which the sweets and cakes are never missing. Her enjoyment would not have been complete without those attendant joys. When the performance was over she sighed and said: 'How I would like to see behind the scenes of a theatre!'

Knowing the author of the play, Mr. Pugh bade her 'Come along,' and rushed her round to the stage-door. There they met most of the actors and the author, who, after a few words of congratulation and explanation, led them behind the scenes.

'Mary Webb drew a deep breath as she stood among the ugly pulleys and general clutter, and clasped her hands together on her breast as if this were a church and she was praying. The back cloth and curtain were up. Presently she wandered away from them on to the stage. She went slowly as far as the footlights and there paused to peer into the dim auditorium. At last she returned laggingly to us as one walking in her sleep, and her face was transfigured as if she had been seeing strange visions in a dream. She said nothing for a while. She maintained an impenetrable silence. . . . Until I took her somewhere for tea, and then she broke into raptures about her peep behind the scenes. The play was as nothing. She seemed to have forgotten all about it. It may be she reflected that the things behind the scenes were real, and those before the footlights false.'

In this, the 'something childish,' Mary Webb's likeness to Katherine Mansfield is again suggested. Katherine Mansfield, too, was never to lose her attitude of wonder towards the simple things. In one of her published letters to her friends she wrote:

'I cannot let Christmas come and go without sending you both my love and greetings. I love Christmas. . . . In that other world, where wishes are laws, there would be a great shining wreath of holly on the door knocker, lights at all the windows, and a real party going on inside. We meet in the hall and warmly re-clasp hands. Good Heavens! *I'm* not above a tree, coloured candles and crackers – are you? Wait. We shall have it all – or something better! . . .'

One who knew Mary Webb intimately writes:

'There was something unearthly about her. She seemed to float like a ghost through the air. . . .

'She was a child, with all a child's shattering shrewdness, outspokenness, insight, vision, and wisdom. She would talk gravely, frankly, innocently, on matters which (in the phrase) are never mentioned. She was unaffectedly, sincerely unconventional.'

A memory remains of Mary Webb at home in Hampstead:

'I often took tea with her and her husband

in their quaintly pretty cottage. Occasionally a visitor would drift in: and then, if he were her sort of man (as she used to say) she would talk. She talked well, but not much. She seemed to prefer to listen. She was so modest, retiring, so unsure of herself that she seemed half afraid to express herself freely . . . except when she was alone with what she called a dear acquaintance, and then she would be at once gravely earnest, almost impassioned, when she was not venting her inborn gifts of immutable wit and humour.'

v

Such was Mary Webb, such were the circumstances of her life, at the time when *Seven for a Secret* was written. The chief distinction of this, her fourth novel, is that its opening chapter is as fine and passionate, as skilful and arresting, as any she wrote before the exceptional opening chapter to *Precious Bane*. It proves her a master of inference, which in this instance she realized is the only possible method of declaring her scene and introducing her characters. It is by inference that we learn of the prosperity of the old farm-house in the midst of Dysgwlfas-on-the-Wild – moors that lay 'between the dimpled lands of England and the gaunt purple steeps of Wales.' We are not told in matter-of-fact phrase that the house was prosperous, but through an attractive word-picture of

'a companionable little township of some five hundred souls – allowing the turkeys to have souls, and including the ewes when they lay near the house at lambing time. As to whether the redpoles, the linnets, and the starlings should be included, Gillian of Dysgwlfas was often doubtful. They sang: they flew: and nobody could sing or fly without a soul: but they were so quick and light and inconsequent, their songs were so thin and eerie, that Gillian thought their souls were not quite real – faery souls, weightless as an eggshell when the egg has been sucked out.'

It is by a similarly romantic statement that we learn why so many domestic preparations are being made at the farm during the afternoon on which the story opens. A group of these five hundred souls, namely the black fantail pigeons, sidled up and down uneasily, troubled all day by the clangour within the house, which, they knew,

'meant some intrusion of the outer world, the world that lay beyond their furthest gaze, into this quiet place, drenched in old silence. It must be that Farmer Lovekin's sister was coming – that Mrs. Fanteague who caused cleanings of the dovecote, whom they hated. They marked their disapproval by flashing up all together with a steely clatter of wings, and surveying the lessening landscape from the heights of the air.'

Even the correct pronunciation of the heroine's Christian name is cunningly inferred. 'By the kitchen table stood Gillian Lovekin. Her full name was Juliana, but the old-fashioned way of treating the name had continued in the Lovekin family.'

The brisk, enthralling movement of this opening chapter is maintained almost throughout the novel, but as in all the writings of Mary Webb, there is very little action. Not yet had the author fully profited by the discovery which comes to all novelists sooner or later, that although the working of the minds of the characters is of supreme importance, its analysis must be revealed not only through outward circumstances but by physical action also. The actual happenings in *Seven for a Secret* comprise little else than a call at a village inn, a journey to the fair, and the visits of an aunt to a niece's home, and of the niece to her aunt in a neighbouring town. The chief incident in the story is a seduction, and the theme is that to which we are by this time accustomed in Mary Webb's novels, the clash of sacred and profane love, symbolized in the relation of Gillian and Robert Rideout and in that of Gillian and Ralph Elmer. Robert Rideout, of the sacred love, is a cowman and shepherd at the farm: Ralph Elmer, of the profane love, is the landlord of a near-by inn whose sign is 'The Mermaid's Rest' but which is familiarly referred to by the local people as 'The Naked Maid.'

' "I dunna like that name. Why dunna they say 'The Mermaid's Rest,' like the sign says?"
' "Well, lad, there she is over the door, shameless as the Woman o' Babylon, mother-naked to the waist. We call her what she is. I'm thankful she's got some decent scales. She's not so ondecent as Eve in my poor mother's Bible. It's little wonder to me as

Adam went wrong. Now if Eve had bought a calico chemise and a pair o' stays and a tuthree petticoats and a nice print dress and apron, there'd ha' been no such May-games with serpents and apples and what not. Maybe their eldest would ha' bin a decent lad and brought up a family close by the old people, and there'd never ha' bin niggers then."

' "Why ever not?"

' "Cain's love-children were the beginning of the niggers." '

Old Jonathan Makepeace is speaking — 'where Jonathan had gained his Scriptural (and apocryphal) knowledge was a mystery' — and in this delightful veteran we have the richest of Mary Webb's numerous comic characters. It is Jonathan Makepeace who lifts the book on to the plane of high and fantastic comedy. Laughter ripples constantly, once we have been introduced to him as 'the most helpless man the woman he married had ever met':

'He was a living illustration of the theory that matter cuts across the path of life. In its crossing of Jonathan's path it was never Jonathan that came off as victor. Jugs flung themselves from his hands: buckets and cisterns

202

decanted their contents over him: tablecloths caught on any metal portion of his clothing, dragging with them the things on the table. If he gathered fruit, a heavy fire of apples poured upon his head. If he fished, he fell into the water. Many bits of his coat, and one piece of finger, had been given to that Moloch, the turnip-cutter. When he forked the garden, he forked his own feet. When he chopped wood, pieces flew up into his face like furious birds. If he made a bonfire, flames drew themselves out to an immense length in order to singe his beard.'

We encounter him first as he comes from shopping, under one arm a bag of chicken-food, under the other a bag of bran; 'both bags, aware of Jonathan, had gently burst, and a crowd followed him with silent and ecstatic mirth while he wandered, dignified and pathetic, towards the inn, with the streams of grain and bran making his passing like a paperchase.' It is drolly in keeping with these pictures of Makepeace that he should argue for the painting out of the wench on the inn-sign at 'The Mermaid's Rest,' or painting a bodice in. 'It draws the eye like that. It's bad for the lads. For until they get married and find out what a poor ornary thing an 'oman is, the lads think she's summat grand and curious.'

Jonathan Makepeace is Robert Rideout's stepfather. And another successful character is Robert's mother, who, as a widow, had decided that Jonathan needed 'mothering' when she saw him during the adventure of the bag of bran and the bag of chicken-food, and married him forthwith. Equally successful in a different way are Fringal, Elmer's ally and attempted blackmailer, who is lost in the dark paths of mental perversion, and Aunt Fanteague, whom the pigeons hated, and who, complained Mrs. Makepeace, 'is never pl'ased. Take your dear 'art out, serve on toast with gravy of your bone and sinew. Would she say thank you? She'd sniff and she'd peer and she'd say with that loud lungeous voice of 'er's, "What you want, my good 'oman, is a *larger* 'art!" '

Then there is Rwth, who is Elmer's secret wife, stolen by him from her gipsy mother, together with much gold, when she was a child of five. Rwth is afflicted with dumbness — even in comedy Mary Webb is unable to conceal her intense awareness of life's tragedy. Rwth stands for the mute suffering of all creation, unreasonable, inevitable — at one crisis in the story 'it was as if there lay across the face of Rwth the perpetual Shadow of the Cross.'

When Gillian's infatuation for Ralph Elmer leads her to Elmer's house she is confronted there by the dumb girl:

'Rwth turned her lustrous eyes upon the intruder, not in surprise but in reverie. She always gave the impression of being impervious to surprise, beyond tears, beyond pain. Her riven young face looked into Gillian's across the mangle. Her spare figure, clad in her usual dust-coloured raiment, with a big sacking apron, her dishevelled hair and arms wrinkled from the wash-tub, would have made her an arresting picture of loveless toil even if she could have spoken.

'But the fact that she could not speak invested her with tragedy. Even to Gillian's unsympathetic, superficial gaze this was obvious. She stood darkly against the whitewashed wall, with the sun smiting across her tired face, and her beautiful eyes dwelt on Gillian's vivid colours.

'Gillian was in sunlight also. The sun seemed to caress her, though it had no caress for Rwth. With her angry flaming cheeks and eyes bright grey with rage, with her richly-tinted dress, her catkins and her red heart, she quite shone against the pale wall. Rwth's eyes lingered on her, accepted her, loved her. Gillian's eyes pitied, Rwth's adored.'

Rwth's devotion to Robert, a frequent visitor to Elmer's inn, is movingly indicated. Each night, when she had taken the pins from her thick, lustreless hair, washed her face and put on her unbleached calico nightgown, she knelt down.

'But the rite she was absorbed in was not that of prayer. Rather it might be called ecstasy. On the bed she had spread out a large red cotton handkerchief of Robert's which he had dropped when helping with the move. She had washed it, ironed it, folded it with sprigs of southernwood and laid it in a drawer.

'Every night she took it out and laid her face upon it, kneeling by the bed. Her dark eye-lashes lay on cheeks flushed with a passion as spiritual and intense as it was unconscious.

'She looked almost beautiful (she could never be pretty or "nice-looking," but just ugly or beautiful) as she knelt so, shaken and flushed with love that was anguish because it had no relief. She could not even speak his name. She could only, with a tenderness that ravaged her face, and yet glorified it, press her cheek hard upon the scarlet cotton decorated with white horse-shoes which Mr. Makepeace thought so delightful a pattern, and which Rwth regarded as a mystic regards his altar draperies – something that had known the sacred presence of the God of Love.'

Gillian knew nothing of the true relation of Ralph Elmer and the dumb gipsy girl who, although wedded to him, has been relegated to the position of drudge. How could she know it, when for Rwth 'to sit and look at Robert was heaven,' 'to hear his voice health and joy,' 'to suffer for him – that was, all unknown to herself, the ultimate purpose of her life'? And when she did suffer, as on the occasion when she saved him from the arduous labour and hurt of cutting the old dog-roses at the expense of a mass of wounds on her hands, she plunged them into the bucket of soda and water to scrub the floor, the smile on her sad face was 'uplifted, ecstatic, as that of a martyred saint.'

Not until after Gillian had yielded to Elmer on the night of the fair did Gillian learn the truth about him. That she could have loved Robert Rideout, the hired man on her farm, at the same time as this happened, has been questioned by the critics. But Mary Webb answers their charge of questionable psychology in a statement that is not only sweeping and uncompromising, but also beautiful and profound in its understanding of men and women:

'In the sifting moonlight brilliant eye met brilliant eye. A vitality greater than their own rushed through their veins and pounded in their breasts. They could no more help themselves than slaves bound for sacrifice on Druidical altars. They were bound for sacrifice on an altar older than mythology: the altar of one who reigns in fold and field, in town and village, in the castle and the hut, who is merciless and arrogant; at once lovely and hideous; who wears the garb of every creed and sect, but belongs to none; who hates virginity; who will be worshipped as long as there remain in the world maids and men; but whose worship is mysterious as the forest, and whose name is unacclaimed of any worshipper — for her name is unknown. She has lust in her treasury as well as love; yet, because of her deathless, keen, miraculous vitality she is clean. And such is her witchery that those who have lived and loved without having known her feel defeated. But those who die in her arms are content as if they already lived in Paradise.'

Ralph Elmer was known to us in the author's gallery of men and women before *Seven for a Secret*. He is the sensual, greedy, callous Reddin of *Gone to Earth*, made living again. The witchery (Mary Webb's phrase) that drew Gillian to Elmer drew Hazel Woodus to Reddin in the earlier book, just as the love which drew Gillian in the end to Robert Rideout is that of Hazel for Edward Marston, or of Jasper Darke for Catherine Velindre in *The House in Dormer Forest*. For a similarity to Gillian we go not to the women who preserve their integrity throughout their time of outward tribulation – it is Rwth who is the noble kinswoman of these – but to a more ignorant and weaker counterpart of them; hardly as fleshy, perhaps, as Lily Huntbatch in *The Golden Arrow*, but resembling her in her inconstancy, her vanity and her cruelty – cold-bloodedly she kills a drake for the sake of the feathers to decorate her hat, and rabbits for their fur. This cruelty is revealed at its worst in the incident of Mr. Gentle, the elderly admirer of her aunt, Miss Fanteague. Gillian deliberately allures him with her more youthful charm and her feminine sophistication into a betrayal of his all-but-declared attitude of love towards Miss Fanteague. She entices him for an outing on the river, and being old and delicate, he takes a chill and eventually dies. This involves the heartbreak of her aunt, who had lived entirely for him and his devotion.

As the outcome of it all we have the ironical vision of Gillian 'in the triumphant beauty of wifehood and motherhood.' The secret that is in the title, or the mystery, is partly revealed in the tragic paradox that those who are all love must suffer, while those who are selfishness, like Gillian, are redeemed. But as to the whole meaning of the secret –

'out in the early summer morning, listening to the silence, you know that there is more, that in and beyond the purple earth and silver sky there is a mystery so great that the knowledge of it would be intolerable, so sweet that the very intuition of its nearness brings tears. . . . It may be that death reveals it. Certainly life cannot, for if we learnt that secret, such is its glory and piercing beauty that it would kill us?

Apart from Jonathan Makepeace, there is in the story only one other personage wholly unfamiliar to those who have approached *Seven for a Secret* chronologically. This is Robert Rideout, to whom Gillian returns after the unmasking of Ralph Elmer, and eventually marries. Robert is a poet as well as a cowman and shepherd. The author draws our attention to this in a manner that strongly recalls the prose-romances of Fiona Macleod.

'And Robert, forgetting that he was only cowman-shepherd, and that Gillian was away, and that there were young men of position in Silvertown, young men whose blood he longed to shed, uplifted his voice and sang:

"She's lying on the white cloud as if it was a bed of flowers.
    If she was asleep, I would kiss her.
    The flowers smell as sweet as a May morning,
    And their petals are as white as milk.
    But her hand's sweeter to kiss and her arm's whiter.

She's like a golden plover running in the
     black yeath —
But when I reach out my hands, she minds
     her as she's got wings.
I've a mind to buy a pair of silver shears
And clip one wing ever so little,
So you couldna fly away from me for ever
     and ever,
Gillian, Gillian, Gillian Lovekin!" '

It is when the association of Elmer and
Rwth is revealed that we begin to feel the loss
of some of the novel's early bloom. There is
rather too much straining after coincidence,
too much borrowing of incidents used in her
earlier books, and this leaves the reader with a
sense of incredulity, which invariably weakens
the hold of a work of fiction. The dumb Rwth,
who is also afflicted with a loss of memory in
regard to her early life, whereby Elmer's hold
on her is strengthened, conveniently remembers the past at a critical moment in the plot,
and we are left questioning. The later incidents
in the book are melodramatic; a feeling of
tiredness creeps into the story as it proceeds, as
though the writing had been done with much
effort. This tiredness leads to superficiality

here and there, and several of the personages are mere sketches instead of complete portraits. Nevertheless it is a noble and beautiful book.

VI

When Mary Webb finished *Seven for a Secret*, towards the end of 1921, she found courage to write to Thomas Hardy and ask his permission that she might dedicate the novel to him. The consequence may be seen immediately following the title-page of the published book: 'To the Illustrious Name of Thomas Hardy, whose acceptance of this dedication has made me so happy.'

When Hardy read the manuscript he must have thought of his own *Far from the Madding Crowd*, which *Seven for a Secret* resembles in some aspects, especially in its charm of pastoral life, and its rustic humour and irresponsibility, so welcome a foil to the dark-hued theme. Mary Webb was never to meet Thomas Hardy. When she was introduced to Mrs. Hardy at the time of the stage-production in London of *Tess of the D'Urbervilles*, she received an invitation to make the journey to his Dorchester home. But the journey was not undertaken, and their meeting never took place.

CHAPTER EIGHT

'Precious Bane' – 'the Sweet in Much Bitter.'

I

MARY WEBB was forty-one years of age in 1922, and by that time she had securely established herself in the esteem of critics and readers of discernment with five books, a collection of nature-essays, *The Spring of Joy*, and four novels, *The Golden Arrow*, *Gone to Earth*, *The House in Dormer Forest*, and *Seven for a Secret*, all published within six years. And yet a letter which she wrote to a fellow-novelist, Mrs. C. A. Nicholson, reveals deep dissatisfaction with her literary progress. She was ailing, and Mrs. Nicholson had expressed the hope that she was receiving adequate medical attention.

'When I have succeeded in getting paid fairly by the British public for my work,' wrote Mary Webb in reply, 'I shall naturally have the best treatment I can get. But not till then. Also, it is less treatment that I want than ordinary good food and a suitable amount of rest and exercise. I have this week existed on bread and scrape and

214

tea. If I give up going to the few things I do go to, I get out of touch with everybody.'

The question (asked in an earlier chapter) why Mary Webb, with a certain amount of financial support assured to her, should have set up a fruit- and flower-stall in Shrewsbury market must now be followed by another: What caused her to write in the strain of the letter just quoted, when, as we have seen, her financial support included publishers' advances which, in the circumstances, were not exactly negligible? The answer is to be found in her character – or, rather, in one especial aspect of it. Miss Hilda Addison, in her short study of Mary Webb's writings and character, has quoted the testimony of relatives:

'Mary's earlier sympathy for the poor and suffering had steadily grown into a veritable passion for giving. If ever a woman knew how "to give and not to count the cost" it was she. No beggar left her unrewarded. Her charity often did more credit to her heart than her head, for she gave extravagantly, with an abandonment which sometimes left her own real necessities unsupplied. A gentle stream of "down-and-outs" discovered Spring Cottage

215

and partook of its mistress's ready charity. They went away with food: they have been known to depart with pound notes. A friend of Mary's said: "She might have twenty pounds in the morning, and hardly ten shillings at night." '

Whatever was asked of her by those who sought her help she joyously supplied. Miss Lory, her friend, has recalled an incident in which a beggar-man and not only food and money play a part, but also two complete outfits of new clothes and shoes for the beggar-man's daughter in order that the girl might be suitably equipped for the situation said to have been awaiting her. Miss Lory has also drawn a charming picture in which Mary Webb may be seen visiting the workpeople's cottages near her home, and asking what the children would like for Christmas. A labourer's daughter, ambitious as well as presumptuous, asked for a piano – and got it! When Mary Webb once received an unexpected windfall of a hundred pounds her immediate impulse was not to save it, but to spend it. And spend it she did, upon a consumptive boy who had caused her anxiety. She arranged for him and his family to be transferred to the seaside from their single room in an East End street. Simply to record these extraordinarily chivalrous actions of hers is illuminating. But any attempt to explain them would be as futile as to seek an explanation why St. Francis devoted so much of his affection to the birds.

Mary Webb's precarious financial state inevitably aggravated her disappointment with the public reception of her novels. The sales had scarcely gone beyond a thousand copies in any instance, despite that early proclamation of her by Miss Rebecca West as a genius. The consequence was that for the novel that came after *Seven for a Secret* she made another change of publishers. They now became the firm of Mr. Jonathan Cape in Britain and Messrs. Dutton & Company in the U.S.A. This novel was not completed until 1924. Thus two years were occupied in the making of her most important work, for the novel was *Precious Bane*.

Partly written at the cottage on Lyth Hill, Shrewsbury, partly at Hampstead, *Precious Bane* came into being under the stimulus of an extremely contrasted environment. In London its author continued to attend literary gatherings and associate with literary people, disappointing and often vexatious though she appeared to find them. Describing in a letter one of her London experiences, she speaks of a function as being 'thick as blackberries with ambassadors, consuls, and such-like people.' During 1924 she found girlish pleasure in acting the part of Madeline in *Nicholas Nickleby* at a Dickens Fellowship Ball, and the photograph taken of her wearing a period dress confirms the recollection by her friends that she made an impression of considerable charm. Of this photograph she had post-card replicas made for Christmas, and that which she sent to Miss Lory conveyed 'love from Gagga.' She also sent a private Christmas card of four pages, bearing a flower design in gold by herself, and signed 'Mary Webb (Mrs. H. B. L. Webb), Five, Grove Cottages, The Grove, Hampstead, N.W.3.' On the inside page was her latest poem, 'The Thornless Rose; a Carol for Peace,' which has not been included in the published collection of her verse:

'Within our hearts a hundred kings,
  With banners like a silver dove,
And gifts of fair and simple things
  Ride out to meet the lord of love.

As Madeleine in Nicholas Nickleby.

Mary Webb
192

MARY WEBB AS 'MADELINE' AT A
DICKENS BALL

'Within our hearts new stars have blazed,
    And over moor and mountain all
The sleepy shepherds hear, amazed,
    Songs like an April curlew's call.

'Now in a world aghast with tears
    A new hope burns, a new faith glows,
From the dark fields of bitter years
    At last there springs the thornless rose.'

Mary Webb was in the mood for writing poetry at that time. For what is *Precious Bane* but poetry, what are the opening pages but lyrical and evocative? As chapter after chapter unfolds, and the narrative sweeps along grandly it is sustained at its highest pitch by a poet's imagery and word-music that make more shadowy than ever the dividing-line between poetry and a poet's prose. Mary Webb poured her full heart into the writing of *Precious Bane*, as though aware that this, above all else, was the reason for her existence, that everything past had been no more than prologue, and that her verses, essays, and earlier novels were but smouldering fires that burst into golden flame at its first note of music – music, like that of Shelley's skylark, 'sweet as love,' *Precious Bane* being above all else a story of love. Not love in its sweetness alone, not only love of humanity, of nature (perfectly conveyed through her prose) but love in its savagery also, its ugly and festering rawness no less than its beauty and holiness. 'For love is a May-dew that can turn the swartest woman to a Jancis' – that is, the most sordid to the most flower-like. But Mary Webb, as we have seen, did not sentimentalize sex.

'And as I saw the squire's shoulders stooped forrard with the weight of his longing I knew for the first time that, whatever my face might be, my body was fair enough. From foot to shoulder I was as passable as any woman could be. Under the red light my flesh was like rose-petals, and the shape of me was such as the water-fairies were said to have, lissom and lovesome.'

In the next passage of the same chapter, that describes the incident of a charlatan's 'Raising of Venus,' all the emotions of thwarted love, love that is withheld, love that is half lust, break forth into a confession by Prue Sarn of her shame that she should have done Beguildy's bidding and pretended to be the naked reincarnation of 'the most beautiful woman that ever was,' – a shame that was 'as if I had gone whoring.' And yet it is not unmixed with rejoicing 'to have given my body in this wise to the eyes of him who was maister in the house of me for ever and ever.'

Chaotic, cruel music as well as sweet and wistful, then: the music, moreover, of a swan song. Mary Webb was writing the last novel she ever completed. And while she wrote it she did not hesitate to turn back in memory to her previous novels, and echoed passages in them, as she needed, in order that the new and nobler creative flame might be fed. 'He's dead, Mother, I'll go and tell the bees, or we met lose 'en,' said Gideon Sarn in *Precious Bane*, echoing Abel Woodus in *Gone to Earth*. Her heart was steeped in remembered loveliness, and what matters if it were sometimes loveliness repeated?

No sooner had she discovered her theme and realized its possibilities than she was convinced that with *Precious Bane* she would reach her highest peak – always a novelist knows when the time has come for the ascent that leads him as near as he will ever be to the stars. In her confident, beautiful foreword she is declaring as clearly as though she actually stated it, the faith that Charles Dickens declares when in the preface to *David Copperfield* he takes the reader 'into his confidence' and tells him that 'of all my books I like this best.' Swan song is a fitting

221

description of *Precious Bane* not only because it proved to be Mary Webb's last completed work, but also because the poetry of it produces music inevitably. It is a note of music that she strikes when at the beginning she describes Sarn, the farm-house in which the story is centred, where 'there's a discouragement about the place. It may be the water lapping, year in and year out — everywhere you look and listen, water; or the big trees waiting and considering on your right hand and on your left; or the unbreathing quiet of the place, as if it was created but an hour gone, and not created for us.' In the oak-wood 'there was always a look of the back end of the year, their young leaves being so brown. So there was always a breath of October in our May' — except on the meadows at Sarn 'when the cowslip was in blow. Gold-over they were, so that you would think not even an angel's feet were good enough to walk there.' The first reference to old Kester, whom the teller of the tale, Prue Sarn, loves and saves and nearly dies for, is made in prose that sounds like a lovely bell: 'Painted butterflies-as-is-to-be, Kester calls them (the caterpillars)' . . . 'Kester's very set about such things. Never will he say caterpillars. He'll say: "There's a lot of butterflies-as-is-to-be on our cabbages, Prue." He won't say "It's winter." He'll say: "Summer's sleeping."' Even the period in which the story is placed – that of the end of the Napoleonic wars when England was a place of spinning-wheels and handlooms, of cockfighting, bull-baiting, wrestling, and the ducking-stool, of people clad in smocks, mob-caps, mittens, sandal-shoes and clogs – even this fact is announced in a passage of sheer poetry:

'And indeed, when I was a young wench there were not many great ladies, even, that could do much more scribbling than to write a love-letter, and some could but just write such things as "This be quince and apple" on their jellies, and others had ado to put their names in the marriage register. Many had come to me, time and again, to write their love-letters for them, and a bitter old task it is, to write other women's love-letters out of your own burning heart.'

In the space of four consummate pages the scene is prepared, and the purpose of the story indicated. It is 'the story of us all at Sarn, of Mother and Gideon and me, and Jancis (that was so beautiful), and Wizard Beguildy, and the two or three folk that lived in those parts.'

The writing of it was encouraged by 'our par-son,' who, 'knowing of the lies that were told of me bade me write all I could remember in a book, and set down the whole truth and nothing else.' The chapter is rounded with a passage so full of vitality and colour and poignant beauty that it will inevitably pass into our per-manent literature:

'Well, it is all gone over now, the trouble and the struggling. It be quiet weather now, like a still evening with the snow all down, and a green sky, and lambs calling. I sit here by the fire with my Bible to hand, a very old woman and a tired woman, with a task to do before she says good night to this world. When I look out of my window and see the plain and the big sky with clouds standing up on the mountains, I call to mind the thick, blotting woods of Sarn, and the crying of the mere when the ice was on it, and the way the water would come into the cupboard under the stairs when it rose at the time of the snow melting.

'There was but little sky to see there, saving that which was reflected in the mere; but the sky that is in the mere is not the proper heavens. You see it in a glass darkly, and the long shadows of rushes go thin and sharp across the sliding stars, and even the sun and moon might be put out down there, for, times, the moon would get lost in lily leaves, and, times, a heron might stand before the sun.'

Mary Webb was well suited by the retrospective, first-person narrative form of *Precious Bane*. She surmounted with remarkable sureness its technical difficulties, preserving and fostering the objective proportion although the dominant note is necessarily subjective. Usually the subjective novelist, as Mrs. Edith Wharton points out in her treatise on *The Writing of Fiction*, lacks the power of getting far enough away from his story to survey it as a whole and relate it to its setting. His minor characters remain the mere satellites of the principal personage, who is, of course, the storyteller, and they vanish when they are not lit up by their central luminary. But Mary Webb's minor characters are always active, though never obtrusive. She has enough energy to spare to win our interest for them. If we were not deeply interested in them we would not be moved, as we definitely are, when towards the end Prudence pauses in her description of the night of grief and fear in which her brother Gideon had 'lost his last game,' and writes: 'Then I thought of golden Jancis and the little babe, and Missis Beguildy, and Father and poor Mother, all dead too. It seemed Death had been very busy at it, swiving among us. Ah! It was a bitter watching, for I ever liked those I cared for to be in good case . . .' The craftsman's self-confidence which is one of the most palpable features of the novel is in every stroke of this reflection. Obviously Mary Webb was taking the reader's interest for granted – and in doing so she was thoroughly justified. The success is the more complete because a novelist's interest in his minor characters inevitably obliges him to include scenes in which they become for the moment more than minor personages. A capital difficulty then arises – how to make it possible in a first-person narrative for the character who tells the story to present with conviction scenes in which he has no cause to be present, or is not present. In the latter case the immediate desire of alert readers is to know by what means the narrator became cognizant of what happened in his absence. And if he is an eye-witness of action and a listener to conversation in which he has no part his presence has to be justified. Astute modern novelists have foreseen the pitfalls of the first-person method and usually avoided it altogether. None of Arnold Bennett's characters, for example, is a narrator, none of his novels a first-person narrative. But Charles Dickens dashed headlong into peril when he chose to make David Copperfield tell his own story, and in this respect one of the great masterpieces of fiction is a grotesque failure. Over and over again David contrives to attend scenes of such intimacy between other personages that his presence is inexcusable, as when on the evening of the departure of Mr. Jack Maldon from Canterbury, Agnes discovers that she has left her little reticule behind and the boy Copperfield runs back to fetch it. The device enables him to witness a scene between Doctor Strong and his supposedly erring wife that is important to the novel in a minor sense, and could not have been introduced except by Copperfield himself. Again, by an obvious device David is taken to Yarmouth so that he might be on the scene of the storm which involves the wreck of the ship on which Steerforth has sailed back to England, and also the loss of Steerforth and Ham, his would-be rescuer. The most grotesque instance of how clumsily Dickens surmounted the first-person obstacle is that of the scene between Rose Dartle and Emily in Martha's lodging. In this case no third person could possibly have been present, or Rose's fierce and merciless denunciation of Steerforth's pathetic victim would immediately have ceased. Dickens, therefore, makes Copperfield play eavesdropper. In the company of Martha he listens, and although all along we have been given the impression that David is a chivalrous young man, he makes not the least attempt to interrupt the agonizing scene. 'Much as I desired to put an end to the interview, I felt that I had no right to present myself: that it was for Mr. Peggotty alone to see her and recover her. Would he never come? I thought, impatiently.' So Emily continues to be tortured that Dickens might redeem his artistry from the inglorious blunder of introducing the scene directly at all. 'Would he never come?' Exactly. We know by that time that even if Rose's blow at the grovelling girl had not merely fallen on the air David would only have gone on murmuring 'Would he never, never come? How long was I to bear this? How long could I bear it?'

Not once in *Precious Bane* does Mary Webb find herself in the slough of artistic error through which Dickens went floundering when he wrote *David Copperfield*. She had realized that the method she was to pursue had its limits: she never permitted her ambition to out-soar those limits by introducing minor plots that would be bound to get out of control. Thus every page of the novel bears sufficient warranty, ample conviction; although it is not gained by narrowing her canvas, which remains large enough to include far more than the huge bulking figure of Gideon, the warlike and masterful farmer, with 'lightning in his blood'; typifying the lust of conquest – in his case the conquest of all that debars him from possession of land and power; primitive, 'beyond good and evil.' Gideon reminds us of Iago, or of the Mayor of Casterbridge, in his fixed idea. It is expressed in actions and reactions ending with his own doom, as well as the doom, through murder and self-destruction, of those who are fated to be near to him.

II

So unerring was the direction in which Mary Webb turned her pen at the outset that instead of finding it necessary sooner or later to lay waste her energy in making her way out of a maze of false positions, she is able to concentrate it. Thus she identifies herself with Prudence Sarn not only in her adventures, but those who have been intimate with the author's personality and other writings before they come to the reading of Prudence's story are unable to resist the thought that a transcended Mary Webb is speaking, pouring out once again her belief in the futility and decay of evil, rooted in materialism, immediately it has to compete with the good rooted in spirituality; proclaiming afresh her sympathy with the bewildered and the lost; proving for the fifth time in her fiction what depth of insight she had into the dark places of the human heart; and repeating her passionate belief that love can make the dark places light.

Especially do we feel this nearness to Mary Webb herself when we learn that Prudence had a physical blemish – symbolical of the ill-health of her creator, and causing her not simply distress but tragic agony. The pendulum of life, however, is for ever swinging. Because the spirit behind Prue's facial disfigurement was the spirit of her creator, it led her to what many regard as the solution of one of the riddles of the universe – the old riddle of suffering, the problem of pain. 'I fell,' said Prue, 'to thinking how all this blessedness of the attic came to me through being curst.' To hide herself she sought the attic at Sarn farm-house, and:

'I had but to creep in there, and hear the bees making their murmur, and smell the woody, o'er-sweet scent of kept apples, and hear the leaves rasping softly on the window-frame, and watch the twisted grey twigs on the sky, and I'd remember it and forget all else. There was a great wooden bolt on the door, and I was used to fasten it, though there was no need, for the attic was such a lost-and-forgotten place nobody ever came there but the travelling weaver and Gideon in apple harvest, and me. Nobody would ever think of looking for me there, and it was parlour and church both to me.'

There it was that 'a most powerful sweetness' would affect her like a great miracle – 'a core of sweetness in much bitter,' and it transformed her life: and 'if I hadna had a harelip to frighten me away into my lonesome soul, this would never have come to me. . . . I should never have known the glory that came from the other side of silence.'

Nevertheless, the harelip could not be forgotten. She is abnormally wistful about it. 'If I do well and go to heaven I shall be made all new, and I shall be as lovely as a lily on the mere. And if I do ill and go to hell, I'll sell my soul a thousand times, but I'll buy a beautiful face, and I shall be gladsome for that though I be damned.' Gideon, partly believing in the terrible superstition then prevalent about a harelip, that it is the sign of a witch, for his own purposes kept his sister well reminded of it.

And when the distressed girl thinks of a plan to rid herself of the disfigurement, by stepping into the mere in the month of August, when the waters were 'troubled,' and, dressed in a white smock, saying prayers in sight of all the folk at the Wake, Gideon denounces the proposal. Their mother, moreover, cries out in support of him: 'What an unkind thing it would be for a poor widow to have it flung in her face afore such a mort of people that her girl had got a hare-shotten lip!'

It was fear and not selfishness that prompted Mrs. Sarn to speak like this. For she is portrayed as an old pathetic woman, eternally haunted by the curse that came to her child and put the 'devil's mark' on her before she had given her birth. 'Could I help it,' she would say plaintively, over and over, 'if the hare crossed my path – could I help it?' Again Mary Webb makes the complete portrait, tender and reminiscent, in a single passage:

'Everything she said, though it might not have anything merry in it, she smiled a bit, in a way you smile to take the edge off somebody's anger, or if you hurt yourself and won't show it. A very grievous smile it was, and always there. So when Father gave Gideon another hiding for wishing he was Beguildy's boy, Mother stood by the table saying, "Oh, dunna, Sarn! Hold thy hand, Sarn!" and smiling all the while, seeming to catch at Father's hands with her soft voice. Poor Mother! Oh, my poor Mother! Shall we meet you in the other world, dear soul, and atone to you for our heedlessness?'

Gideon, too, is presented to us by his sister with a quaint half-worshipful, half-fearful charm. His name, to begin with, was 'one you couldn't shorten':

'You can make most names into little love-names, like you can cut down a cloak or a gown for children's wearing. But Gideon you could do nought with. And the name was like the man. I was more set on my brother than most are, but I couldna help seeing that about him. If nobody calls you out of your name, your name's like to be soon out of mind. And most people never even called him by his Christian name at all. They called him Sarn. In Father's life it was old Sarn and young Sarn.

'But after Father died, Gideon seemed to take the place to himself. I remember how he went out that summer night, and seemed to eat and drink the place, devouring it with his eyes. Yet it was not for love of it, but for what he could get out of it. He was very like Father then, and more like every year, both to look at and in his mind. But that he was less tempersome and more set in his ways, he was Father's very marrow.

'Father's temper got up despert quick, and when it was up he was a ravening lion. Maybe that was what gave Mother that married-all-o'er look. But Gideon I saw only angered, to call angered, three times. Mostly, a look was enough. He'd give you a look like murder, and you'd let him take the way he wanted. I've seen a dog cringing and whimpering because he'd given it one of those looks. Sarns mostly have grey eyes – cold grey like the mere in winter –

and the Sarn men are mainly dark and sullen. "Sullen as a Sarn," they say about these parts.'

At the outset this sullenness of the Sarns has caused the death of Gideon's father. The children have played truant from church in order to play 'conkers,' and they borrowed their version of the sermon from one who had attended, a child named Tivvy whose stupidity directly leads to the tragedy.

' "Now, tell!" says Gideon. So she began to cry, and said she knew nought about it. Then he twisted her arm, and she screamed out, "Burning and fuel of fire!"

'She must have said that because it was one of the texts the Sexton was very fond of saying over, keeping time with tapping his staff the while.

' "What else?"

' "Nought."

' "I'll twist your arm till it comes off if you dunna think of any more."

'Tivvy looked artful, like Pussy in the dairy, and said –

' "Parson told about Adam and Eve and Noah and Shemamanjaphet and Jesus in the manger and thirty pieces of silver."

'Gideon's face went dark.

' "There's no sense in it," he said.

' "But she's told you, anyway. You must let her go now."

'So we went home, with the shadow of the spire stretching all across the water.

'Father said —

' "What was the text?"

' "Burning and fuel of fire."

' "What was the sarmon about?"

'Poor Gideon made out a tale of all the things Tivvy had said. You never heard such a tale! Father sat quite quiet, and Mother was smiling very painful, standing by the fire, cooking a rasher.'

The humour of this scene, deliciously exploited, provides a telling contrast to the sombreness of the happening that follows:

'Suddenly Father shouted out —

' "Liar! Liar! Parson called but now, to say was there sickness, there being nobody at church. You've not only taken dog's leave and lied, but you've made game of *me*."

'His face went from red to purple, and all veined, like raw meat. It was awful to see. Then he reached out for the horsewhip and said —

' "I'll give you the best hiding ever you had, my boy!"

'He came across the kitchen towards Gideon.

'But suddenly Gideon ran at him and bunted into him, and taking him by surprise he knocked him clean over.

'Now whether it was that Father had eaten a very hearty supper, after a big day's work with the bees, or whether it was him being in such a rage, and then the surprise of the fall, we never knew. He never stirred, but lay on his back on the red quarries, breathing so loud and strong that it filled the house, like somebody snoring in the night. Mother untied his Sunday neck-cloth, and lifted him up, and put cold water on his face, but it was no manner of use.'

Thus it was that Sarn farm-house came into the possession of seventeen-years-old Gideon. Not by inheritance, however, did he gain his ownership, but by a deliberate gesture at the graveside of the dead man. In her preface to the novel Mary Webb has prepared the reader for a 'sin-eating,' —

'Now it was still the custom at that time, in our part of the country, to give a fee to some

237

poor man after a death, and then he would take bread and wine handed to him across the coffin and eat and drink, saying –

' "I give easement and rest now to thee, dear man, that ye walk not over the fields nor down the byways. And for thy peace I pawn my own soul." '

Sin-eaters having become scarce, Gideon offers to soothe his mother's uneasy, superstitious mind by becoming the Sin-Eater. But the 'strange, heart-shaking thing' does not come to pass until Gideon has seized his opportunity and clinched the grim bargain:

'He took up the little pewter measure full of darkness, and he looked at Mother.

' "Oot turn over the farm and all to me if I be the Sin-Eater, Mother?" he said.

' "No, no! Sin-Eaters be accurst!"

' "What harm, to drink a sup of your own wine and chumble a crust of your own bread? But if you dunna care, let be. He can go with the sin on him."

' "No, no! Leave un go free, Gideon! Let un rest, poor soul! You be in life and young, but he'm cold and helpless in the power of Satan. He went with all his sins upon him, in

his boots, poor soul! If there's none else to help,
let his own lad take pity."

'"And you'll give me the farm, Mother?"

'"Yes, yes, my dear! What be the farm to
me? You can take all, and welcome."

'Then Gideon drank the wine all of a gulp,
and swallowed the crust. There was no sound
in all the place but the sound of his teeth biting
it up.

'Then he put his hand on the coffin, standing
up tall in the high black hat, with a gleaming
pale face, and he said — *"I give easement and rest
now to thee, dear man. Come not down the lanes
nor in our meadows. And for thy peace I pawn my
own soul. Amen."* '

There is perhaps no more masterly stroke in
the book than the 'aside' of Prudence Sarn
which follows: — 'But when Gideon said,
"Come not down the lanes nor in our
meadows," I thought he said it like somebody
warning off a trespasser.' The neatest minor
strokes are in the description of how their playmate Jancis had 'got a way of saying "O" afore
everything and it made her mouth look like a
rose, but whether she did it for that or whether
she was slow-witted and timid I never could

tell': and in the grim humour of Gideon's shout to the rooks in the elm-trees at Sarn – 'Ho, rooks! Father's dead, and I be maister, and I've come to say as you shall keep your housen in peace, and I'll keep you safe from all but my own gun, and you're kindly welcome to bide.'

But perhaps the outstanding neatness of stroke is in the lighter humour that flashes upon Gideon's thunderous commands when, youthful master of Sarn, he outlines to Prudence their future in which he is to be a rich man and his sister a rich lady:

. . . ' "And I'll be churchwarden and tell the Rector what to do, and say who's to go in the stocks, and who's to go in the almshousen, and vote for the parliament men. And when any wench has a baby that's a love-child, you'll go and scold her."

' "I'd liefer play with the baby."

' "Anybody can play with a baby. None but a great lady can scold. And we'll buy a grand house. I hanna put my eye on one yet, but there be time enow. And a garden with a man to see to it, and serving-wenches, and the place full of grand furniture, and silver plate and china.'

' "I dearly like pretty china," I said. "Can

we get some of them new cups and saucers from Staffordshire, with little people on 'em?"

' "You can get anything you like, and a gold thimble and a press full of gowns into the bargain. Only you mun help me first. It'll take years and years."

' "But couldna we stop at Sarn and get just a little bit of new furniture and china, and do without so many maids and men?" '

In this last faint protest by Prudence Sarn, desiring only quietness and simplicity, we are given the leading theme of *Precious Bane*. It is that of the 'old ancient charm' called content, and how Prudence learnt it – not from books, but through Nature and a brave man's love – so that it worked within them both, until materialistic circumstance, outward event, physical manifestation became as nothing apart from the life of spirituality.

'For I do think,' was Prue's conclusion, 'that the spirit makes herself busy about the body, and breathes through it, and throws a veil over it more fair than it is of itself. For what is flesh alone? You may see flesh alone and feel nothing but loathing. You may see it in the butcher's shop cut up, or in the gutter, drunken, or in

the coffin, dead. For the world is full of flesh
as the chandler's shelf is full of lanthorns at the
beginning of winter. But it isna till you take
the lanthorn home and light it that you have
any comfort of it.'

III

Gideon too was a dreamer. But it was by a
very different road from that which Prudence
travelled that he followed his dream. Two or
three times in his life, as his wise, discerning
sister observes, he was given the opportunity
to take the good road — 'the path of love and
merry days, where the pretty paigle grew, the
keys of heaven' — meaning the cowslips — and
instead he chose 'the path of strange twists and
turns, where was the thing of dread, the bane,
the precious bane, that feeds on life-blood.'

Into his dream came the lust of material gain,
of power and possession, of all that brings about
the inevitable tragedy in human existence. And
woven inextricably into Gideon's dream-net was
Jancis, whom we envision at first as the little
playmate of the Sarns, Jancis of the golden hair,
'and all the shadows on her face seemed to be
stained with the pale colour of it'; Jancis, with

242

the red cool smiling mouth, 'and when she smiled the dimples ran into each other.' 'Times I could almost have strangled her for that smile,' recalled Prudence: but it was not Prue Sarn that strangled her and her baby in the end, but the mere, with its lily leaves and its thin sound of bells, that the children used to think were the bells of a village down under, but which were only the echo bells from the neighbouring church. The last time we see Jancis is alongside Gideon, who is saying farewell to her:

'The night afore we took them to the church-yard I heard him stirring, and being afraid that in a sudden horror of the spirit he might do himself a mischief, for though a slow, quiet man in daily life, he could be, now and again, hasty of a sudden, I went to see what the matter was.

'He was standing beside the bed. As I went in he had just stretched forth his hand and lifted in his great brown fingers the plait of golden hair, so thick and fine, that was ever the pride of poor Jancis. When he turned at my coming, he was like a lad taken in a fault, hanging his head and muttering, as if it should explain his act, which indeed it did — "I did love her once." '

It is not on this sombre note that the story of

Prudence Sarn reaches its conclusion. Kester has broken in upon a grim scene, dominated until his coming by terrible voices, 'Suffer not a witch to live!' 'Tromple on her!' 'Stone her!' 'Let her drown!' They seemed in the ears of the terrified woman with the hare-shotten lip, at whom they were directed, 'like the blaring of some great demon.' And breaking in upon this awful moment there came to her rescue the man Kester, whom she had met first at Jancis's love-spinning, but whom she felt so powerless to describe that she gives instead the words of the coarse and sensual Felena:

'Felena drew me farther from the rest.

' "A man," she said, "whose like I've not seen afore, neither on the roads nor at market. The others are gaubies to him. Did you see the colour of his eyes?"

' "No."

' "Nor could I see. His eyelids cut across them so straight, and the candle of his eye is so big and black, you canna see the colour. I'd lief be nigh him, to see."

'Her glass-green eyes misted, and a rich, swooning look came over her.

' "A man to gamble for," she said. . . .

'As I sat down I twisted the words of Felena in my mind, and said in the deeps of myself —
'"Not a man to gamble for. A man to die for."'

The revelation to Kester that here was his 'angel,' and to Prudence that she it was whom he thought of, though she considered herself 'a poor daggly sort of angel,' came to them at the end of the most thrilling incident in the story, that of Prue's rescue of Kester from a horrible death at a bull-baiting. And at the close of the book, after innumerable obstacles, Kester Woodseaves and Prudence Sarn, now rescued in her turn from the ducking-stool, ride together away from superstition to security, away through the evening wind that lifts the boughs 'like a lover lifting his maid's long hair,' strong in their faith in a life beyond the actual, in which hare-shotten lips fade to nothingness, and the hidden glory of love outshines everything. The horseman is refusing to listen to the plea of the rescued woman he has lifted into the saddle — 'just as in a dream I had,' thinks Prue; but no, he must 'marry a girl like a lily,' not one who is 'hare-shotten.' 'I've chosen my bit of Paradise,' he answers, and then, in the quaint lovely accent of the place and period, "Tis on your breast, my dear acquaintance.'

CHAPTER NINE

*The Last Phase – A Prime Minister's Tribute –
An Unfinished Novel – And Her Art Reviewed*

I

MARY WEBB'S principal novel, *Precious
Bane*, was published in July, 1924, less
than a year after *Seven for a Secret*. It is not
difficult to imagine the eagerness with which
she awaited the first reviews. True, a few
months earlier she had revealed her disillusionment about contemporary authorship in a
scornful passage:

'To-day the craft of letters has been turned into
a strictly commercial transaction, and books are
manufactured with the prompt neat aplomb of
a pot of factory jam. Those must have been
great days when it was a hall-mark of nobility
to have written a book; when nobody wrote
except for the love of it; when no mediocre
work was turned out. Greater days still when
it might mean martyrdom to have written a
book; when the whole life and soul of a man
went into it, freighting it with such beauty and
wonder that it would defy the centuries. Have

246

we lost the art of distillation by which the spirit was rendered to an essence and preserved in an indestructible form?'

Being human, however, she could not help feeling anxious about the fate of her own authorship, in these supposedly less great days. We can picture her turning to one of the leading literary journals, hurriedly scanning it for a review of *Precious Bane*: we can understand her feelings as she reads the following words:

'This is a pleasantly ambitious work of fiction. But it is not sufficiently in the spirit of our time to awaken more than a "literary" interest in the reader.'

And here is an evidently well-considered criticism in another of the weekly reviews, and therefore worthier of our attention:

'The chief obstacle to a full acceptance of Mrs. Mary Webb's novel *Precious Bane* is not so much that it is written in a highly poeticized Shropshire dialect but that it is supposed to be narrated by an ill-educated country woman who found time to keep a diary during a life of hard work on a farm. It requires a deal of imagination to believe that Prue Sarn, however straight the furrows that she ploughed, would be likely to write:

'"And I knew it would take a heap of money to cure a hare-shotten lip. There was a kind of sour laughter in the thought of it. It called to mind the blackish autumn evenings when grouse rise from the bitter marsh and fly betwixt the withered heather and the freezing sky, and laugh. Old harsh men laugh that way at the falling down of an enemy. And the good ladies of a town, big with stiff flounced silks and babes righteously begotten, laughed so behind their fans when they went to the prison to see a lovely harlot whipped."

'However, those who accept the figment that Prue had a cultivated mind and a power of expressing it in words, as well as a noble spirit, will find here a good story. It is a romance of the Shropshire countryside, without any nonsense in its humanity or sentimentality in its love-making. The tragedy of Gideon Sarn, Prue's brother, is classic in its lines. . . . Not only is the drama well-arranged and convincing in its outlines, but it is very pleasantly diversified with descriptions of old Shropshire scenes and customs.'

The belated tribute to the author's treatment

of Gideon Sarn and his tragedy as 'classic in its lines,' apart from which there is no indication in this influential review that the novel is in any way out of the common ruck, fails to minimize the earlier strictures, or redeem their essential fallacy. There is no warrant for the statement that Prue Sarn is an ill-educated countrywoman. Of 'humble station,' as she herself confesses, yes! But at the very outset it is made to appear perfectly natural that she received 'book-learning,' and when, after Beguildy had 'learned me to read and write and reckon up figures,' Gideon suggested that his sister should learn to do sums and keep accounts and write, she was glad, 'for I dearly loved the thought of being able to read books, and especially the Bible.' And when the reviewer expresses scepticism as to the likelihood of Prudence having the power of highly poeticized writing, we think of Pippa, the little silk-winder in Robert Browning's poem who passed from one scene to another and unconsciously touched the less coarse sensibilities of one group of holiday-makers after another by the songs which she carolled in the spring sunshine. As Professor H. B. Charlton has emphasized, Pippa does not sing 'It is springtime,' but 'the year's at the spring,' catching just that infinitesimal instant of time when the air is filled with all that is meant by the coming of spring. She also sings 'The hill-side's dew pearled.' Truly this ignorant workgirl, whose life of toil is only relieved by one annual holiday, is endowed with a miraculous speech, a gift of tongues! This is entirely legitimate for artistic purposes; but in case a distinction is claimed between Pippa singing and Prudence writing, we will add that it was also legitimate for another great writer to put these words into the mouth of a crude Highland chieftain:

'If it were done when 'tis done, then 'twere well
It were done quickly. If the assassination
Could trammel up the consequence, and catch,
With his surcease, success; that but this blow
Might be the be-all and the end-all here,
But here, upon this bank and shoal of time,
We'd jump the life to come. . . . I have no
    spur
To prick the sides of my intent, but only
Vaulting ambition, which o'erleaps itself,
And falls on the other.'

If Shakespeare had the right to endow Macbeth — and even the murderers, attendants, and messengers at Inverness Castle – with the gift of speaking blank verse nobly, and playing most skilfully on his words (and nobody has denied him), then it is equally legitimate for Mary Webb to endow Prudence Sarn with what is a far more natural gift, not of speech, but of writing down her thoughts in a fashion more plausible than the reviewer allows when he wrongly refers to 'a diary which she found time to keep during a life of hard work on a farm.'

'As soon as I could write,' explains Prue, 'I made a little book with a calico cover, and every Sunday I wrote in it any merry time or good fortune we had had in the week, and so kept them. And if times had been troublous and bitter for me, I wrote that down too and was eased. So when our parson, knowing of the lies that were told of me, bade me write down all I could remember in a book and set down the whole truth and nothing else, I was able to freshen my memory with the things I had put down Sunday by Sunday.'

How disappointed Mary Webb must have been with this inadequate review can only be properly understood by a creative artist who has poured out his best energies and maturest years of life into such an ambitious book as she had written. She knew that certain reviewers had a habit of taking their cue from this particular journal. So indeed they did, as it proved, in the instance of *Precious Bane*. There were a few exceptions, however, one of them being the late Edwin Pugh, who had courageously and persistently pressed the claims, one after another, of her two preceding books. Mr. Pugh roundly declared *Precious Bane* to be a masterpiece, and he wrote that

'Mary Webb has a style of exquisite beauty which yet has both force and restraint, simplicity and subtlety. She has fancy and wit, delicate humour, and pathos of the finest and most delicate, almost subliminal gifts of characterization and visualization – she sees and knows men aright, as no other English woman novelist does: she can, moreover, tell a story and so intrigue you with its sense of inevitableness that it seems more real than reality. She has, in short, genius.'

But Edwin Pugh's voice cried in the wilderness, and Mary Webb plaintively confessed to a friend some time after the appearance of *Precious Bane* that the novel had up to then not sold more than 1,200 copies. Mr. Pugh did not grow weary, however. He was the principal actor in an unexpected and extraordinary scene — indeed, he was its hero — at a literary function, which Mary Webb attended in his company. The star of the evening was described by Mr. Pugh as 'a woman-novelist who had done excellent work and reaped her full reward in praise and pence.' The hall was packed from floor to platform, and although Mr. Pugh was able to find seats for his wife and Mary Webb, he had to sit on the floor. From that lowly place he heard speaker after speaker not only 'beslaver' the novelist who was the guest, but almost every other popular woman novelist. He waited in vain to hear the name of Mary Webb — she who, in his firm belief, was the greatest of them all. He could tolerate it no longer. He scrambled to his feet and told a surprised audience that though the women novelists who had been mentioned by name were all worthy of respect, there was a far greater novelist than any of them, 'and her name,' he shouted, 'is Mary Webb.' . . . Away at the back of the hall Mary Webb was weeping on his wife's shoulder for sheer joy in that heroic outburst, 'while I' (again to use his own words) 'was back in my lowly place on the floor, wondering if I had made a colossal ass of myself.' And, he grimly added, when recalling the scene later: 'Fortunately she was too excited, after that, to heed or even hear the few tepid sentences of the faint praise that spells damnation which followed my outburst.'

II

Edwin Pugh had not made a 'colossal ass' of himself. He was a gallant champion, and with his memory must always be associated not simply the books he himself wrote so honestly and worthily, but his effort preceded a recognition of Mary Webb. For in the spring of 1925, nearly a year after the publication of *Precious Bane*, she received notification from the 'Femina Vie Heureuse' Committee, appointed to discover the best imaginative work in prose or verse descriptive of English life by an author who had not gained sufficient recognition, that her novel had been awarded their prize for 1924–5.

St. John Adcock recalled the presentation ceremony. 'I attended on that occasion,' he wrote. 'Her husband and her brother, newly

254

returned from India, came with her. And her undisguised delight in it all was, I am sure, unalloyed by any thought of how much good work she had had to do before that honour fell to her.' Mr. Adcock's impression of Mary Webb was of 'a small, frail person, with large anxious eyes and a manner in which shyness and a hesitant sort of self-confidence were curiously mixed.' She made a 'pleasant little speech,' it is also remembered, and 'she wore a heliotrope dress with a belt on which she had embroidered fleurs-de-lys as a compliment to the French donor.'

Her mother's death took place in 1925. She joined her brothers and sisters for the funeral at Chester. In *Precious Bane* she had written: 'Poor Mother! Oh my poor Mother! Shall we meet you in the other world, dear soul, and atone to you for our heedlessness?' The two had not lost touch with one another, although they lived apart since her marriage. Her mother was sometimes a visitor to the cottage on Lyth Hill. It was she, indeed, who testified to the intensity with which her daughter wrote her books by humorously complaining that when she stayed with her she could never be sure either of a meal unless she got it herself or of even gaining entrance to the cottage. About his sister's intensity during composition Captain Douglas Meredith has declared: 'I have seen her sitting on a 'bus going to Shrewsbury, with a pad on her knee and writing throughout the journey.'

The loss of her mother had an adverse effect on her always precarious health and her spirit. She was at the beginning of a new novel, but she was now so dependent on her moods that sometimes she did not write a line for several weeks. She relieved her inactivity by contributing short stories and reviews to the London periodicals.

III

Precious Bane had now been published eighteen months. Probably she was resigned to its disappointing reception when, at the beginning of 1927, a letter reached her from the Prime Minister of England, addressed to the care of her publishers. The letter was dated from 10 Downing Street, Whitehall, January the 14th:

'DEAR MRS. WEBB,

I hope you will not think it an impertinence on my part if I tell you with what delight

I have read *Precious Bane*. My people lived in Shropshire for centuries before they migrated to Worcestershire, and I spent my earliest years in Bewdley, which is on the border. In your book I seem to hear again the speech and turns of phrase which surrounded me in the nursery. I think it is a really first-class piece of work and I have not enjoyed a book so much for years. It was given to me by one of my secretaries and I read it at Christmas within sight of the Clee Hills, at home. Thank you a thousand times for it.

'Believe me to remain,
'Sincerely yours,
'STANLEY BALDWIN.'

Her reply, dated from Hampstead eleven days later, follows:

'DEAR MR. BALDWIN,
    'Thank you very much indeed for your most kind letter which I received last Tuesday. That the man with least leisure, I suppose, of anybody in the British Empire should spare time to write me a letter with his own hand about my book, has delighted and touched me very much. That one notably versed in the classics should find my style pleasant is a feather

in my cap. That a personality of so much breadth and vigour should find my ideas worth reading, is perhaps best of all. I shall have pleasure in asking your acceptance of the book I am now writing, which is about the Welsh Marches just after the Norman Conquest, when Bewdley, as I expect you know, was a famous City of Refuge for people fleeing from the depredations of the Lords Marchers. I hope it will be published this Spring. It is nice that you read *Precious Bane* within sight of those enchanted hills. Please accept a little bunch of violets for your writing-table. I am sending them to-morrow.

'Yours sincerely,
MARY WEBB, MRS. H. B. L. WEBB.'

A postscript was added: 'I am very much obliged to your Secretary.'

IV

At that time, after nearly two years' work, the new novel to which she referred in this letter was still barely half done. It was left to St. John Adcock to tell of the melancholy outcome. As editor of the *Bookman* Mr. Adcock added his encouragement to that of her other admirers – it was in the pages of this monthly that Edwin Pugh wrote his praise of her works – and upon a fellow-writer of such ready sympathy and friendship as Mr. Adcock she naturally called with the news of the Prime Minister's letter. Mr. Adcock confessed that 'having acquired a dreadful business instinct' he urged her to write and ask Mr. Baldwin's permission to print that letter in an advertisement: but 'being highly nervous and possessing no professional instinct, she was horrified at the suggestion. He might not like it. He might take offence at such a request. She could not think of such a thing. . . .' And so the matter was left. . . . Not long afterwards St. John Adcock was called up on the telephone, and she was at the other end, in evident distress. She began saying something about how very unwell she had been, and added abruptly: 'I have destroyed all I had done of the new novel.'

'There was no immediate answer to my exclamations,' said Mr. Adcock, 'and I have seldom heard anything more piteous than the subdued, stifled sound of her crying at the other end of the line. Presently, when she could speak again, she blamed herself, but said she had been so dissatisfied, felt she could not finish it, and would never write any more, so, on a sudden impulse, had torn the MS. and put it on the fire. Before we finished talking she was reconciled to making the best of things, said she could recall it nearly all word for word, and would at once set about re-writing it.'

Unknown to her, the manuscript had been rescued from the flames, so that she was not called upon to undergo the tremendous effort of re-writing the story. But when she left London for Shrewsbury in the spring she had added hardly anything to the work, and it remained a fragment, unpublished until after her death, when it appeared with ten characteristic short stories. So it stands, as *Armour Wherein He Trusted*, which had originally been 'A Strong Man Armed,' until the author learnt that a novel already published in the U.S.A. forestalled her in the use of the title. As she explained to Mr. Baldwin, it is a story of the Welsh Marches just after the Norman Conquest, told like *Precious Bane* in the first person. The narrator is Lord Gilbert of Polrebec, afterwards the Holy and Pious Abbot of Strata Florida, and again the theme is war between the flesh and the spirit. The deliberate artificiality and archaisms of the style are managed with a success which promises a triumph as significant as that of *Precious Bane*:

'All was still – still as a dewpond. The great oaken boughs were a little leafy with young red leaves, and they spread and towered in the quiet, minding them of the centuries, aye, minding them of the hour that was so still, a thousand years gone and more, when the midnight grew sudden-sweet and small flowers were where had been none, and bells spoke in the meady, golden air, and the thin echo of voices came upon the land:

' "Pax vobiscum! Christus natus est."

'The oaks called it to mind. Though storms ravened, they seemed ever at their orisons, and never did I come there but a stillness fell upon me. My good horse stopped, snuffling the air, staring, sweating, then hung his head, hearing as I know well, beneath the sea-voices of the high boughs – "Christus natus est."

'I left him standing there and went softly on, over the stag-moss. All was so holy, I was glad I was dressed in my best green coat and my hat with a grey goose feather, for it was as if I went to the Easter Supper.

'After a while, I saw that in the midst of this oak grove was a thicket of Christ-thorn, bravely budded. So I went into the thicket, thinking I might find an altar there. But there was no altar, only a small bower woven of wattles and decked out with bunches of early flowers – marigolds and the flowers of young hyacinthus, and the day's eye. Small nimble birds made claw-marks in the soft earth about it, and the merles sang as if none but faeries ever came there.

' "It is a witchen-house," I said. "I shall be put in a spell." And even as I spoke, one looked from the small window of the bower, and behold! it was my love. I knew it was my love, though I had never seen her afore, and I was bewildered, standing like an oaf, looking upon her under the leaves. I mused on her long, struck, as the heron is when he sees his mate imaged in the water. She seemed not troubled at all to have a great fellow standing there, and by this I was sure she was a faery, since they know not fear.

' "Alas!" I said, "I am a man doomed for I love a faery, an Ill Person."

'Then on a sudden she laughed, high and

brisk, yet with a sound of rain going in the trees. And she rose up and came stooping from the low door, and stooping looked up at me from under her forehead with its clumps of pleated golden hair on this side and on that side. So looking up while yet her chin nestled against the sheepskin of her coat, her face, that was pointed, like one of the Small People's faces, seemed even more pointed, like some forest creature – a scurrel, say, or a fox-babe or a vole. Then she straightened and stood like a wand, solemn, as one offended. And she said –

' "Sir, I am no Ill Person. I am my Lady Powis's new waiting-woman out of Wales, where are no tall tousle-haired gentlemen that stare upon a maid in her bower."

'And turning aside, she seemed to be looking very carefully at the small clouds that came over the tree-tops each after other, like ptarmigan in winter. So I fell into a muse also, for it seemed that there was no other thing any lady could do so fitly as to watch the white ptarmigan in the meadows of God. And I mind this was ever her manner – to make all she did seem the only thing that could be done. For if she leaned over the battlements, or stirred simples over the hearth fire, or sewed her tapestry, it seemed to all that she could do none other thing. And if she sate at the banquet, she seemed in a shrine as if a great boss of white roses was her chair-back. Never did I see any woman so favouring Our Lady.

'So a man coming on a dark night to a church with a bright painted window such as they have in Rome, seeing the Mother of God done in lovely blues and raddles, would say "Ah me! when was the Flower of the West in holy Italy?" For that was her name – leastways among men. Women had other names for her. But men called her ever "Flower of the West," and indeed she was at that time, and to me at all times, the fairest woman from Chester to the Southern Sea. Men would fight for a look and die for a smile. But that was after. On this day she was yet a very simple maid, and abashed.'

Mr. Martin Armstrong, in his introductory note to the published volume, suggests that if the reader stops reading a few pages before the fragment actually breaks off, *Armour Wherein He Trusted*, as it stands, is a story complete in itself. That is at the point when the struggle for mastery between the two loves, mortal and immortal, had resolved itself, the mortal love having prevailed, and Nesta won as his wife. But then the immortal comes to him with irresistible force: the peace of his home – exquisitely conveyed – is destroyed by one who had been discovered lying across the threshold, 'twisted and lean and brown, with his ribs standing out, and his hair long and wild as pine boughs,' and who seemed to Gilbert 'as if the wooden Christus had come down from the wall staring upon us with cavernous eyes.' The call had come for Gilbert to follow Peter the Hermit to the First Crusade.

'He lifted up his lean, long arm, and the cresset flaring behind him set its gnarled shadow on the other wall.

'He set his devouring eyes upon me.

' "Young man," he said, "I say unto thee, arise and come. The Lord hath need of thee."

'At these words there came a shriek from where my mother was, so sharp it seemed it must have cut her heart in two.

'We stared upon the man.

' "Gilbert Polrebec," he said in his strange tongue, mingled of Saxon and some country French, "I come from Peter Hermit. Thou must return with me now, swiftly, for because of his old kindness for thy mother he wills that thou go with him in this first glorious Crusade, walking beside him as his own familiar friend. Multitudes that none can number will be about thee, marching Godward, and if thou diest there will be a seat for thee in the innermost circle of the heavens at God His elbow."

' "Cruel and evil one!" shrieked Nesta, and rushing at the man she smote him on the face with a litten torch.

'I put my arms about her to restrain her. But it seemed the man cared no more for blazing torches than for wolves. He went on speaking, calm as a Mass-thane in his own chapel, though the hot pine-resin had seared his cheek all across.

'My father meanwhile sat down heavily in his chair, as if his knees would not uphold him.

' "If thou wilt not leave father and mother and wife, housen and lands, thou art not worthy of me, saith the Lord."

'My father spoke, but his voice was hoarse and shaken as an old man's voice.

' "The lad is but young, sir."

' "We desire the young," the man replied.

' "And lately wed."

' "In heaven is no marrying nor giving in marriage."

' "And we be ageing folk, his mother and my own self, and we have ill-wishers and we need our son."

' "The Lord hath ill-wishers also in all the towns of Galilee, and He commandeth Gilbert Polrebec to fight in His behalf."

Doubts assail Gilbert, and a great perplexity.

'Seeing him stand afore the image of our Lord, it seemed that my thoughts grew moithered, so I could not tell which was the stranger and which was Christus, or whether Christus had been in peril of wolves and recovered by Gudrun, or whether the one that summoned, speaking with so stern a voice, summoned in truth from the comfortless tree that hung upon the wall.'

But the doubts are dramatically swept away. For

'turning anywhere to save me from his eyes, that caught me and lured me into a spell of terror I looked toward the Christus on the wall.

'And behold, a dreadful marvel! For even as I looked, the image shuddered and two tears rolled down the face, and He did bat His eyes at me. And when I saw the Lord God so shuddering and weeping upon our wall, and when, in the manner of some poor babe denied of some sweetmeat or some revel, He did so bat His eyes and droop His head, I knew that I must go, and my heart turned in my side and my soul uttered a cry, and I forgot myself, falling on darkness.'

Then comes the passage referred to by Mr. Martin Armstrong as a fitting end.

'And so in the grey dawn we departed, leaving the castle all blinded and folded in mist, and the litel grey garden blotted out, and those three beloved ones weeping and groaning at the door where I was to go in and out no more until many a year was fled. But in the wan light of morning I saw that the Christus on the rood wept no more, nor batted His eyes, but seemed more at ease, satisfied as a child at some promise long withheld but at last given.'

v

The same critic classifies *Armour Wherein He Trusted* as

'a curiously complete fragment that takes its

place in her work as a brief excursion into a narrower and more self-conscious form. It is a carefully wrought tapestry, its designs highly artificial and full of calligraphic detail, its grey and silver background thickly strewn with bright and dancing colours. It is as if a modern painter of the country, such as Constable, were to have devoted himself for once to the illumination of a missal.'

The comparison of painting is a sound one, although we doubt if time would have proved the work to be a 'brief excursion.' . . .

We are lingering now for the last time on Mary Webb's writings, and if we recall them as a whole we shall perceive that the comparison might have been applied from the beginning. She was always a painter of the country. She was always something else. She worked with the consciousness that, as she suggests subtly in the novels and states with directness in her essays on Beauty, Joy and Laughter, to the 'patient watcher of earth' suddenly there comes 'a clapping of wings, a flash of immortal radiance, a strange haunting cry – and he has had a vision of the Soul of the World.' In this passage she re-emphasized the vital principle to which Plato, dreaming in Old Greece, was probably the first who gave clarity, and on which art ever since has been based – that Nature is not a chaos, but a Harmony. The artists themselves may often be unconscious of it, just as humanity itself is often unconscious, but dimly groping, nevertheless, for the key that unlocks the world. Into the hands of each one of us, even the humblest, even the visionless who see Nature only as red in tooth and claw, that key is given – in a sunset, maybe, or a passage of sublime music, or even the music of a barrel-organ in a drab street – cheap mechanic music suddenly transformed by some mysterious alchemy of the mind into what the poet Mr. Alfred Noyes describes as a harmony that 'surrounds the singing organ like a large eternal light.' The little silk-winder of Asolo, in Robert Browning's poem, held the key that Easter morning when she broke into a happy song that ended with the esctatic declaration, 'God's in His Heaven, all's right with the world.' No longer was she humble, a dweller in sordid surroundings, a mere workgirl who had set out to make the most of her only holiday in all the year, but a visionary, a natural mystic, to whom life, with its perfections and imperfections, had become the 'grand, harmonious, universal orchestral movement.' 'The Maister be come.' Mary Webb suggested this state of absolute loveliness in a passage describing how 'out of the mud that seems so ugly, up the green rushes comes the delicate dragon fly, and sets the air on fire.' It is in such flashing half-moments as Browning knew, and Mary Webb knew, and all the poets and artists — half-moments that inevitably leave the heart numbed and empty with a sense of Paradise Lost once more after being Paradise Regained — that the world is unlocked, and fulfilled is the universal human desire for a glimpse of 'that subtle beauty which lies beyond the rim of the sky.' Sir Thomas Browne believed that 'we live the life of plants, the life of animals, the life of men, and at last the life of spirits,' and it is during the keen and startling recognition of our 'oneness with all beauty, seen and unseen, that those whose everyday existence is that of plants, animals and men at last live the life of spirits.' Then, as Mary Webb wrote in her little book of essays, 'we are in complete communion with the universal life. The winds are our playfellows; Sirius is our fellow-traveller; we are swept up into the wild heart of the

271

wild. Then we know that we are not merely built up physically out of flower, feather, and light, but are one with them in every fibre of our being.' We pause to reflect how inevitable was her humane attitude towards all living things – the identical attitude that was shown by Robert Louis Stevenson when, as we are told by his biographer, he saw a dog being illtreated, and interposed, saying to the owner, who resented his interference: 'It's not your dog, it's God's dog, and I'm here to protect it.' . . .

Mary Webb continues:

'Then only do we have our full share in the passion of life that fills all nature; then only do we possess perfect vitality. Then we are caught into the primal beauty of earth, and life flows in upon us like an eagre. Life – the unknown quantity, the guarded secret – circles from an infinite ocean through all created things, and turns again to the ocean.'

Out of this miracle is born the mystic: hence, each in a degree, all men and women are mystics, and it is precisely because our being is completely identified with the mystical life for only one flashing moment now and again that we are at the mercy of outward tribulation. The true way, the salvation of mankind, therefore, lies in the subjugation of all that ends this moment of unity, all that makes for misunderstanding and perplexity; and the seeking and finding of spiritual security.

Thus Mary Webb was nearer to being a complete mystic than the majority of men and women. This did not prevent her from sharing the paganism of Richard Jefferies, and the double rôle does not seem paradoxical when we remember that Jefferies wrote such a book as *The Story of My Heart*. Like Jefferies, she had more than the ordinary human share of communion with the universal life. And it was the passionate longing to share her experience of that 'miraculous sweetness' that was the motive of her writing. It is redundant to say, as her critics have said, that she was a mystic first and a novelist only afterwards — that 'when all is said and done, there is little doubt that she will be remembered in after years, not as a great novelist, but as a woman with the soul of a poet and the observation of an artist.' How may craftsmanship take priority over imagination and emotion? It is because a writer is predominantly a mystic — or, as may happen, predominantly a materialist – that he is impelled to take up his pen. He cannot assume – convincingly, at any rate – an attitude when his pen is already in his fingers.

It seems curious to those who believe Mary Webb to be a major novelist that there are others who deny her the title of novelist at all, and ask us to be content to think of her as one possessing the 'soul of a poet and the observation of an artist.' Not so many mystics have written worthy novels that we can afford to be disparaging about one who could write them with great distinction. She put her visionary experience, her perception of what complete mysticism may mean, to very proper and welcome use when she was led to write about human beings, for the danger of writing an abstract treatise is that it may result in nothing more than an additional strengthening of the general suspicion that mysticism is a vague and formless refuge from reality.

Ernest Renan said: 'We ought never to write except about the things we love. Silence and oblivion are the reward we mete out to everything that strikes us as unlovely or ignoble on our journey through life.' It was her impulse to write novels that saved her from this negative attitude. She perceived that nothing is artistic-

274

ally unlovely or ignoble, everything is lovable and lovely, when the artist is in perfect concord with the universal life. Each of us, artist and 'commoner,' apart from the complete mystic (who is as rare as the complete non-mystic), has been unable in some measure to nourish and develop to its highest what Mary Webb calls 'the triune capacity for loving his fellow and nature and the Creator of them,' that has been implanted in everybody.

'These loves may be latent, but they are there: and unless they are all developed we cannot reach perfect manhood or womanhood. For the complete character is that which is in communion with most sides of life – which sees, hears, and feels most – which has for its fellows the sympathy of understanding, for nature the love that is without entire comprehension, and for the mystery beyond them the inexhaustible desire which surely prophesies fulfilment some-where.'

VI

Mary Webb preferred fiction, because it was in her novels that she was best able to portray the incomplete character, the hurt and suffering creatures who are victims of a lack of spirituality; and to narrate their struggle against circumstance. She was obsessed with the battle of good and evil, with the flashing half-moments of divinity and the world that dispels them. Gideon and Prudence Sarn in *Precious Bane*, Edward Marston and Hazel Woodus in *Gone to Earth*, Deborah Arden and Stephen Southernwood in *The Golden Arrow*, Jasper and Amber Darke in *The House in Dormer Forest*, Gillian Lovekin and Robert Rideout in *Seven for a Secret* — all of these characters, some of whom have lost their spiritual integrity and others who have retained it in spite of the material forces that can so easily lead to loss, are the embodiment of the incomplete divinity in human nature. Not only Prudence Sarn among Mary Webb's creations learnt where to find 'the core of sweetness in much bitter'; others besides Gideon Sarn turned to 'the path of strange twists and turns, where was the thing of dread, the bane, the precious bane, that feeds on life-blood.' Many a novelist who is not content to be only a teller of tales spends his imaginative energy in subtly contrasting the futility and decay of evil, rooted in materialism, with the peaceful security of good. That he will do so with pity and understanding is to be taken for granted. That he is himself in some degree a mystic is also to be taken for granted. Mary Webb claimed for the mystic that he 'understands sex better than the sensualist. . . . He can analyse greed, hypocrisy, better than those who swim obscenely in their own black passions. . . . A saint and not a devil can best unravel the psychology of evil.' As novelist then, Mary Webb helped to re-establish the one great purpose of the novel – to present actual life in its eternal clash between spirituality and materialism. In this lies her contribution to twentieth-century literature. She brought to English fiction some rare qualities, those which are all too often lacking in the novelist. She had the love of earth, epitomized in one special corner of earth: a profound faith in men and women, epitomized in the diverse group who peopled the Shropshire she wrote about: a profound consciousness of the importance of scenery and natural beauty in their lives: and an exquisite sense of style.

She recognized that the use of words is as vitally important in prose as in poetry. 'What echoes are in them of bygone labour and achievement,' she exclaimed: 'of yellow harvests, of axes barking in the forest, of rickyards, and spacious kitchens lit by the Christmas faggot!' Her knowledge of the true meaning of art saved her from extravagances of language. In *Precious Bane*, which is narrated by one who speaks in dialect, it is only occasionally that a dialect word is employed, yet the style has all the rich suggestiveness of idiomatic speech. Rarely, moreover, is the dialogue distorted:

' "You be above yerself, woman. You think to see our Jancis wedded and bedded and rounding to a grandchild all in a lantern-puff. But I tell ye not every troth ends in church, not every ring holds wedlock, not every bridegroom takes his vargin, and I dunna like the match! Owd Sarn still begrutches me that crown, though he be where crowns buy nought. And I tell you young Sarn was born under the threepenny planet and 'll never keep money. Sleeps on his face too. And them as does that drowns. My gel's not for Sarn. You may ride roughshod over my wish and will. You may send out bidding letters for a love-spinning, which is all to the good. But still I'll bide for a higher bidder. Why, she be as white as a lady and as sound as a well-grown tater! No squire nor lord even but ud take it kind to be asked to lie beside her." '

The writer of that passage knew that the only way to avoid misuse of dialect is by idiomatic suggestion rather than literal transcription. Expression in art is essentially suggestion, and the artist's task is to convey dialogue by the use of a word whose effect is broadspread, or by a turn of phrase; not by consistent misspelling and distortion. Mary Webb's triumph in this aspect of style is all the more emphatic to those who remember how as 'regional' novelists Robert Louis Stevenson and J. M. Barrie misused dialect. It is a triumph that might easily have been a defeat as noticeable as theirs, for she must have been sorely tempted by the apple-like quality of local words, their richness and roundness. 'How these words and phrases chime and murmur!' she exclaims in reference to another novelist's writing. And again: 'The geography of words is a fascinating study. One finds that in mountain country a word in daily use on one side of a range will be non-existent on the other. Even in the plains words will fade away suddenly, like the fringes of a rain-storm.'

In style, then, as in her quick sense of dramatic values, her humour, and her profound love of earth and the children of earth, Mary Webb is an authentic novelist, for all these combine to create a feeling that her novels belong to the people, that they were not given life by an author, but that they live with the unconscious inevitability that belongs to growing things. 'The hero of a country story,' she would say, in discussing her art, and it might have been her great forerunner, Emily Brontë, who was speaking, 'the hero of a country story must be instinct with the countryside: it is in his very bones. So it must always be in a novel that attempts the interpretation of earth through character. For the dwellers in mountain and forest are under this burden, that they must unconsciously express those dumb masses and forces that have no other voice than theirs. No novel of the countryside can attain greatness unless it unifies its characters with the earth, half frustrate, half triumphal.' Nor, we may continue, is it robbed of its greatness if the novelist has no originality of plot. That situations are repeated in Mary Webb's novels with their resemblance only slightly concealed may seem a drawback, and the fact has been eagerly seized upon. But plot-making belongs to invention rather than imagination. Few novelists are imaginative as well as inventive; criticism of a similar lack of invention in

Thomas Hardy has long been silenced, and it is by the tremendous fact of his imagination that this silence has been enforced. When we consider what the ability to invent plots might have cost in reduced imaginative energy in the case of Mary Webb, we readily grant that she lacks originality as a story-teller, at the same time rejoicing that it has ensured to us such passages as this, from *Gone to Earth*:

'It was as if the dead had arisen in the stark hours between twelve and two, and were waiting unobtrusively, majestically, each by his own bed, to go down and break their long fast with the bee and the grass-snake in refectories too minute and too immortal to be known by the living. The tombstones seemed taller, seemed to have a presence behind them: the lush grass, lying grey and heavy with dew, seemed to have been swept by silent passing crowds.'

Or this, from *The House in Dormer Forest*:

'The bracken waved wild arms in beautiful abandon, not quite of summer, but not yet tinted by autumn, having attained the transparent golden-green that comes before the burning colours of September. As she walked, she watched the misty plain. Away in the east, where the land was cold and low, it seemed as if the sky had fallen – as if she was looking down on the mysterious upper sides of the clouds – thick, lavish, of a weighty whiteness. . . . To the west the mist thinned and was like pale water. Upon it, with delicate dignity, the trees floated, like water-birds of faery, gravely and magically tinted. Some were brown-green, like grebes, others of the ashy tint of coots, the soft grey of cygnets. The chestnuts, where the sun struck them, were like sheldrakes with their deep bronzes; and the beeches had the glossy green of teal. The white sea was populous with these fairy creatures, floating head under wing.'

Or this again from *Gone to Earth*:

'For as yet spring had no flight, no song, but went like a half-fledged bird, hopping tentatively through the undergrowth. The bright springing mercury that carpeted the open spaces had only just hung out its pale flowers, and honeysuckle leaves were still tongues of green fire. Between the larch boles and under the thickets of honeysuckle and blackberry came a tawny silent form, wearing with the calm dignity of woodland creatures a beauty of eye and limb, a brilliance of tint, that few women could have worn without self-consciousness. Clear-eyed, lithe, it stood for a minute in the full sunlight – a year-old fox, round-headed and velvet-footed. Then it slid into the shadows.'

Instead of invention Mary Webb had the imagination of genius: imagination sweetened in love, and this brought her as near to the understanding of what life is most real, 'this wholly mysterious life that moves unseen through the world,' as any woman novelist of her generation. Her creative instinct forbade her to waste more than the minimum of energy on technicalities, although her craft is not unworthy of that creative instinct; and consequently she was able to come near to knowing, and also to teaching us, through her lovely writings, what she knew about 'this mysterious life that moves unseen through the world.' She advanced sufficiently towards the heart of its secret to perceive that beauty, joy and laughter are the necessities of our being, as all her writings emphasize: and that if we lose contact with these three things we lose our hold on life, and on eternity.

HER final writing was done while she was in Shropshire during the summer of 1927. It was a review of a novel by Mrs. Edith Wharton, and it contained these sentences: 'After all, who is afraid of a dead leaf in winter? Only in the rose-gardens of summer is it a threat.' . . . She returned to London in September. Looking back towards home from the speeding train she lost the Wrekin in mist as the quiet village of Shifnal flashed past, and more than dimly she perceived even then that she might find her 'enchanted hill' no more. For autumn had fallen upon Mary Webb also; her ill-health was aggravated by an accident at the Hampstead cottage – a trivial tumble which nevertheless gave her a shock from which she made only a slow recovery. As the summer drew to its close there was that in her manner, and indeed in her movements, which made plain to understanding eyes that her hold on life was precarious. She would stand where the little gate led out from the garden of Spring Cottage to the open hillside; she beheld that vast Shropshire panorama of mountains and valleys, and now it was her own created world;

284

but she must have known that every day brought her mortal contact with it nearer an end.

When she reached London her friends perceived that the only course left for her was to cast off, if possible, the dispiriting memories of disappointments and disillusionments that so often attend a literary career. . . . 'You must go away. You must not work. There must be a complete break with all your old surroundings.' . . . And she yielded. She thought of Miss Lory, her oldest and still her most intimate friend, who was now living at St. Leonards-on-Sea. She expressed a desire to be near her, and by the end of September she had made her departure from the cottage at Hampstead. A friend companioned her railway travelling, but in response to her entreaty ('so that Miss Lory might not be alarmed') alighted from the train at the first of the two stations in St. Leonards, and left her to complete the journey alone. Miss Lory was alarmed just the same. For the exertion had been too much for the stricken woman, and Miss Lory's first glimpse was of an exhausted, limp figure being carried from the train by the railway officials. Immediately Miss Lory decided to take her to a nursing-home instead of her own house on West Hill. Mary Webb rallied by the time she arrived. She was delighted with her room, at the top of the building, looking out over the sea. She moved across to the window before she could be persuaded to get into bed. The pale gold of a September sunset was glorious on the water. 'Oh, how beautiful,' she exclaimed. 'I shall get better quickly here.' But then she turned away, and as they helped her into bed she buried her face in the pillows and cried.

Never did Mary Webb show her great fondness for flowers so touchingly as in the days that followed. She would gather her favourite violets into her cupped hands and kiss them and snuggle them against her throat. Her pleasure was great when her husband brought lilies from her own plant in London – he had been privately advised to come, although she had not intended that he should be interrupted in his work. Her thoughts lingered lovingly on Nature, her last solace. Her brother Douglas, then stationed in the South, was sent for, and when he arrived her whispered greeting was: 'Hello, Duss, are the leaves turning yet?'

Two mornings later, when Miss Lory arrived at the bedside and placed a bunch of violets in her hand and told her that they would all have tea together in the afternoon, she smiled faintly, and managed to whisper: 'That will be nice.' Those were the last words she uttered; softly she fell into sleep – the hour was noon – and by two o'clock she had passed away without waking.

Mary Webb died of pernicious anæmia and Graves's disease on Saturday, October 8th, 1927. She was taken to Shrewsbury for her burial. Nearly seven months later, on April 25th, 1928, the Right Hon. Mr. Baldwin made a speech at the Royal Literary Fund annual dinner. He recalled that he read *Precious Bane* at Christmas, 1926, and had been so impressed by the novel that he mentioned the author to Sir James Barrie and Mr. John Buchan, who told him that 'she is about one of the best living writers, and no one buys her books.'

He went on to express surprise that a novelist of genius should have been so neglected that her death passed unnoticed in the newspapers. This was substantially true. Only four papers may be excepted from Mr. Baldwin's statement. And in spite of the esteem in which certain of her fellow-writers held her, and of the tribute paid to her by the Femina Vie Heureuse Prize

Committee, with the exception of *The Golden Arrow* and *Precious Bane* her books had been allowed to go out of print.

The immediate effect of Mr. Baldwin's words was that the voices of the critics were suddenly raised in a chorus of belated adulation. The reading public, whose imagination is unfailingly touched by the phrase 'neglected genius,' began to read her novels with such enthusiasm that quickly she became a 'best seller.' Truly 'success' at last was hers.

But Mary Webb, sleeping among her well-beloved hills, the 'hills of home,' has been magnificently unconcerned about it all. Once she petitioned in a poem:

> 'Under a blossoming tree
> Let me lie down,
> With one blackbird to sing to me
> In the evenings brown.'

For there, she felt, she would sleep sound, safe from the world's 'blames and praises.'

THE END

A LIST OF BOOKS IN

THE TRAVELLERS' LIBRARY

at 3s. 6d. net each

THE LIFE AND LETTERS SERIES

at 4s. 6d. net each

AND OF VOLUMES PUBLISHED IN THE
UNIFORM EDITIONS OF THE WORKS OF

RADCLYFFE HALL
SINCLAIR LEWIS
MARY WEBB

AND

E. H. YOUNG

at 5s. net each

JONATHAN CAPE
THIRTY BEDFORD SQUARE LONDON

A NOTE ON THE ARRANGEMENT
OF THIS CATALOGUE

The main body of the list is arranged alphabetically under the names of AUTHORS. In addition, for the convenience of readers, there is an index at the end giving the titles of all books included in this catalogue arranged alphabetically and there is also an index of titles arranged according to their numbers in each series.

The Travellers' Library contains books in all branches of literature, fiction and non-fiction, poetry and prose, copyright and non-copyright. The series is designed for the pocket, or for the small house where shelf-space is limited. Special care has been taken with the production of each volume, type, paper and binding having all been chosen with this end in view, and at the same time made worthy of the books selected.

Note

The Travellers' Library is published as a joint enterprise by Jonathan Cape and William Heinemann. The series as a whole, or any title in the series, can be obtained from any bookseller. In any case of difficulty application should be made direct to either Jonathan Cape, London, or William Heinemann, London.

ANDERSON, Sherwood
HORSES AND MEN. Stories   *No.* 54
'*Horses and Men* confirms our indebtedness to the publishers who are introducing his work here. A man of poetic vision, with an intimate knowledge of particular conditions of life here looks out upon a world that seems singularly material only because he unflinchingly accepts its actualities.' *Morning Post*

ANONYMOUS
ENGLAND'S GREEN AND PLEASANT LAND   *No.* 161
A study of rural life. 'His picture is vivid, vivacious, scintillating, and behind it is the busy brain of the reformer, the warm heart of the true lover of his kind.' *Manchester Guardian*

2

ARMSTRONG, Martin

THE BAZAAR. Stories   *No.* 77

'These stories have considerable range of subject, but in general they are stay-at-home tales depicting cloistered lives and delicate, finely fibred minds. . . . Mr. Armstrong writes beautifully.' *Nation and Athenæum*

ATKINS, J. B.

SIDE SHOWS. Essays. With an Introduction by

JAMES BONE   *No.* 78

Mr. J. B. Atkins was war correspondent in four wars, the London editor of a great English paper, then Paris correspondent of another and latterly the editor of the *Spectator*. His subjects in *Side Shows* are briefly London and the sea.

AUSTEN, Jane

NORTHANGER ABBEY. With an Introduction by

REBECCA WEST   *No.* 182

'It is characteristic of Jane Austen's art that she presents this story, which was the fruit of strong feeling and audacious thought, with such perfect serenity that one accepts it as a beautiful established fact.' *From the Introduction*

BARING, Maurice

HALF A MINUTE'S SILENCE. Stories   *No.* 153

Tales from Russia, some of them accounts of real happenings; ghost stories, school stories, classical inventions, character sketches, fairy tales and parodies, legends and romances.

BATES, H. E.

THE TWO SISTERS. A Novel   *No.* 160

MR. EDWARD GARNETT in his foreword to *The Two Sisters* says: 'A novel of rare poetical order . . . . his achievement is that, while identified with his creations—Jenny, Jessie and Michael —the author has known how to detach himself from these figures of eternal youth and show them, with all their tumultuous, passionate emotions, in a beautiful mirror.'

BELLOC, Hilaire

SHORT TALKS WITH THE DEAD   *No.* 79

In these essays Mr. Belloc attains his usual high level of pungent and witty writing. The subjects vary widely and include an imaginary talk with the spirits of Charles I, the barber of Louis XIV, and Napoleon, Venice, fakes, eclipses, Byron, and the famous dissertation on the Nordic Man.

BENNETT, Arnold

THE OLD WIVES' TALE. Two volumes   *Nos. 166 and 167*

'All attempts to sum up his merits and measure his achievement must rest upon *The Old Wives' Tale.*' *The Times*

BERCOVICI, Konrad

BETWEEN EARTH AND SKY. Stories of Gypsies.

With an Introduction by A. E. COPPARD   *No. 117*

Konrad Bercovici, through his own association with gypsies, together with a magical intuition of their lives, is able to give us some unforgettable pictures of those wanderers who, having no home anywhere, are at home everywhere.

BIERCE, Ambrose

CAN SUCH THINGS BE ? Stories   *No. 1*

'Bierce never wastes a word, never coins a too startling phrase; he secures his final effect, a cold thrill of fear, by a simple, yet subtle, realism. No anthology of short stories, limited to a score or so, would be complete without an example of his unique artistry.' *Morning Post*

THE MONK AND THE HANGMAN'S DAUGHTER. Written in collaboration with

ADOLPHE DANZIGER DE CASTRO   *No. 34*

'These stories are evidence of very unusual powers, and when once they have been read the reader will feel himself impelled to dig out more from the same pen.' *Westminster Gazette*

BIRON, Sir Chartres

' "SIR," SAID DR. JOHNSON—'. An Anthology   *No. 184*

In ' *"Sir," Said Dr. Johnson—*' the traveller, whether he is realizing 'the grand object of travel' in 'seeing the shores of the Mediterranean' or 'raising his children to eminence' by 'viewing the Wall of China,' will find both sympathy and entertainment, nor need he be deterred under modern conditions by the Doctor's 5th rule of Travel 'Get a smart seasickness if you can.' Here in a handy form will be found an anthology of the great lexicographer's invigorating reflections on men and matters.

BIRRELL, Augustine

MORE OBITER DICTA   *No. 140*

'Age has not wearied Mr. Birrell's humour; nor have the years condemned his whimsicality. He remains as delightful a companion as ever.' *Nation and Athenæum*

BOURGOGNE, Sergeant

MEMOIRS OF SERGEANT BOURGOGNE. With
an Introduction by SIR JOHN FORTESCUE *No.* 148

It is vivid from the first page to the last and the subject, the Retreat from Moscow, is unexampled in its horrors. Bourgogne is French of the French—a typical soldier of the Guard, brave, quick-witted, resourceful, gay and humane.

BOURNE, George

A FARMER'S LIFE *No.* 32

The life-story of a tenant-farmer of fifty years ago in which the author draws on his memory for a picture of the everyday life of his immediate forbears, the Smiths, farmers and handicraft men, who lived and died on the border of Surrey and Hampshire.

BRAMAH, Ernest

THE WALLET OF KAI LUNG *No.* 18

'Something worth doing and done. . . . It was a thing intended, wrought out, completed and established. Therefore it was destined to endure, and, what is more important, it was a success.' HILAIRE BELLOC

KAI LUNG'S GOLDEN HOURS *No.* 16

'It is worthy of its forerunner. There is the same plan, exactitude, working-out and achievement; and therefore complete satisfaction in the reading.' *From the Preface by* HILAIRE BELLOC

BRONTË, Emily

WUTHERING HEIGHTS *No.* 30

'It is a very great book. You may read this grim story of lost and thwarted human creatures on a moor at any age and come under its sway.' *From the Introduction by* ROSE MACAULAY

BROWNE, Lewis

THE STORY OF THE JEWS *No.* 146

Here is a history which is more absorbing than any work of fiction. The author traces the beginnings of the Jewish race from the wandering Semitic races of Arabia, through interminable strife, oppression, expatriation, up to modern times.

BUTLER, Samuel

EREWHON. A Satire   *No. 11*

'Occasionally, very occasionally, a bit of genuine satire secures for itself more than a passing nod of recognition. *Erewhon* is such a satire. . . . The best of its kind since *Gulliver's Travels*.'
AUGUSTINE BIRRELL

EREWHON REVISITED. A Satire   *No. 12*

'He waged a sleepless war with the mental torpor of the prosperous, complacent England around him; a Swift with the soul of music in him, and completely sane; a liberator of humanity operating with the wit and malice and coolness of Mephistopheles.' *Manchester Guardian*

THE NOTE BOOKS   *No. 75*

'The freest, most original and most varied thinker of his generation. . . . Neither *Erewhon* nor *The Way of All Flesh*, but the posthumous work entitled *Note Books* will stand, in our judgment, as the decisive contribution of Samuel Butler to the thought of his age.' *Nation*

SELECTED ESSAYS. This volume contains the following essays :   *No. 55*

THE HUMOUR OF HOMER	HOW TO MAKE THE BEST OF LIFE
QUIS DESIDERIO . . . ?	THE SANCTUARY OF MONTRIGONE
RAMBLINGS IN CHEAPSIDE	A MEDIEVAL GIRLS' SCHOOL
THE AUNT, THE NIECES,	ART IN THE VALLEY OF SAAS
AND THE DOG	THOUGHT AND LANGUAGE

THE WAY OF ALL FLESH. A Novel   *No. 10*

'It drives one almost to despair of English Literature when one sees so extraordinary a study of English life as Butler's posthumous *Way of All Flesh* making so little impression. Really, the English do not deserve to have great men.' GEORGE BERNARD SHAW

CANOT, Theodore

MEMOIRS OF A SLAVE TRADER. Set down by BRANTZ MAYER and now edited by A. W. LAWRENCE   *No. 126*

In 1854 a cosmopolitan adventurer, who knew Africa at the worst period of its history, dictated this sardonic account of piracy and mutiny, of battles with warships or rival traders, and of the fantastic lives of European and half-caste slavers on the West Coast.

CARDUS, Neville
DAYS IN THE SUN: A Cricketer's Book   No. 121
> The author says 'the intention of this book is modest—it should be taken as a rather freely compiled journal of happy experiences which have come my way on our cricket fields.'

CARLETON, Captain George
MILITARY MEMOIRS (1672-1713). Edited by
A. W. LAWRENCE   No. 134
> A cheerful sidelight on the war of the Spanish Succession, with a remarkable literary history. Johnson praised the book, Scott edited it, and then the critics declared it to be fiction and suggested Defoe or Swift as the author; now it has come into its own again as one of the most vivid records of a soldier's actual experiences.

CATHER, Willa
THE SONG OF THE LARK   No. 183
> *The Song of the Lark* is the story of an American opera singer, her childhood in the Colorado desert, her early struggles in Chicago, her romantic adventures among the Cliff Dweller ruins in Arizona, her splendid triumphs on the operatic stage. There is a diverting picture of musical circles in Chicago. There are wonderful chapters of the Cliff Dweller ruins which first awake in the heroine the historic imagination so necessary to a great Wagnerian singer, and where she grows all at once into a powerful and wilful young creature, gets her courage, and begins to find herself.

CLEMENTS, Rex
A GIPSY OF THE HORN. Life in a deep-sea sailing ship   No. 136
> A true and spirited account of a phase of sea-life now passing, if not passed, fascinating from the very vividness and sincerity of its telling. Mr. Clements loves the sea, and he makes his readers love it.

COLLETT, Anthony
THE CHANGING FACE OF ENGLAND   No. 177
> 'His knowledge of the English countryside is extraordinary; he can not only name the trees and flowers, the birds and beasts of every district, but he can tell what every village is built of and why.' *The Manchester Guardian*

COPPARD, A. E.

ADAM AND EVE AND PINCH ME. Stories   *No. 13*
Mr. Coppard's implicit theme is the closeness of the spiritual world to the material; the strange, communicative sympathy which strikes through two temperaments and suddenly makes them one.

CLORINDA WALKS IN HEAVEN. Stories   *No. 22*
'Genius is a hard-ridden word, and has been put by critics at many puny ditches, but Mr. Coppard sets up a fence worthy of its mettle. He shows that in hands like his the English language is as alive as ever.' *Outlook*

FISHMONGER'S FIDDLE. Stories   *No. 130*
'In definite colour and solid strength his work suggests that of the old Dutch Masters. Mr. Coppard is a born story-teller.' *Times Literary Supplement*

THE BLACK DOG. Stories   *No. 2*
'Mr. Coppard is a born story-teller. The book is filled with a variety of delightful stuff: no one who is interested in good writing in general, and good short stories in particular, should miss it.' *Spectator*

COYLE, Kathleen

LIV. A Novel. With an Introduction by REBECCA WEST   *No. 87*
'*Liv* is a short novel, but more subtly suggesting beauty and movement than many a longer book. . . . There is something cool and rare about this story; the reader finds himself turning back to re-read pages that must not be forgotten.' *Times Literary Supplement*

DAVIES, Charles

SELECTIONS FROM SWIFT. With an Introduction by
CHARLES DAVIES   *No. 171*
Everybody knows *Gulliver* and *The Tale of a Tub*, but Swift's minor pieces are less accessible in a handy format. In this book a collection of the more interesting will be found, exhibiting the Dean in familiar and satiric mood even when preaching.

DAVIES, W. H.

THE AUTOBIOGRAPHY OF A SUPER-TRAMP
With a Preface by G. BERNARD SHAW   *No. 3*
The author tells us with inimitable quiet modesty of how he begged and stole his way across America and through England and Wales until his travelling days were cut short by losing his right foot while attempting to 'jump' a train.

8

DAVIES, W. H.

LATER DAYS. A pendant to *The Autobiography of a Super-Tramp*   *No.* 48

'The self-portrait is given with disarming, mysterious, and baffling directness, and the writing has the same disarmingness and simpleness.' *Observer*

A POET'S PILGRIMAGE   *No.* 56

A Poet's Pilgrimage recounts the author's impressions of his native Wales on his return after many years' absence. He tells of a walking tour during which he stayed in cheap rooms and ate in the small wayside inns. The result is a vivid picture of the Welsh people, the towns and countryside.

DELEDDA, Grazia

THE MOTHER. A Novel. With an Introduction by
D. H. LAWRENCE. (Awarded the Nobel Prize 1928)   *No.* 105

An unusual book, both in its story and its setting in a remote Sardinian hill village, half civilised and superstitious. The action of the story takes place so rapidly and the actual drama is so interwoven with the mental conflict, and all so forced by circumstances, that it is almost Greek in its simple and inevitable tragedy.

DE MAUPASSANT

STORIES. Translated by ELIZABETH MARTINDALE   *No.* 37

'His "story" engrosses the non-critical, it holds the critical too at the first reading. . . . That is the real test of art, and it is because of the inobtrusiveness of this workmanship, that for once the critic and the reader may join hands without awaiting the verdict of posterity.' *From the Introduction by* FORD MADOX FORD

DE SELINCOURT, Hugh

THE CRICKET MATCH. A Story   *No.* 108

Through the medium of a cricket match the author endeavours to give a glimpse of life in a Sussex village. First we have a bird's-eye view at dawn of the village nestling under the Downs ; then we see the players awaken in all the widely different circumstances of their various lives, pass the morning, assemble on the field, play their game, united for a few hours, as men should be, by a common purpose — and at night disperse.

DIMNET, Ernest
THE ART OF THINKING
No. 170

'Concentration, "never reading but always studying," dismissing trivialities and only reading masterpieces, orderliness, taking notes, avoiding laziness—it is with such aids to improving the mind that M. Dimnet chiefly deals—and the point of his witty book is that he makes such difficult operations seductive by the charm with which he surrounds both the operations themselves and the results to which they should lead.' *The Times Literary Supplement*

DOS PASSOS, John
ORIENT EXPRESS. A book of travel
No. 80

This book will be read because, as well as being the temperature chart of an unfortunate sufferer from the travelling disease, it deals with places shaken by the heavy footsteps of History. Underneath, the book is an ode to railroad travel.

DOUGLAS, George
THE HOUSE WITH THE GREEN SHUTTERS
A Novel. With an Introduction by J. B. PRIESTLEY *No. 118*

This powerful and moving story of life in a small Scots burgh is one of the grimmest studies of realism in all modern fiction. The author flashes a cold and remorseless searchlight upon the back-bitings, jealousies, and intrigues of the townsfolk.

DU MAURIER, George
PETER IBBETSON. Illustrated by the author
No. 169

This novel, written as an autobiography, reveals with a pathetic charm the figure of Peter Ibbetson from boyhood. Some of the scenes are English, but most of the story is in France, the early part of it in Passy and Paris.

DUNSTERVILLE, Major-General L. C.
STALKY'S REMINISCENCES
No. 145

'The real Stalky, General Dunsterville, is so delightful a character that the fictitious Stalky must at times feel jealous of him as a rival. . . . In war he proved his genius in the Dunster Force adventure; and in this book he shows that he possesses another kind of genius—the genius of comic self-revelation and burbling anecdote.' *The Observer*

FARSON, Negley

SAILING ACROSS EUROPE. With an Introduction
by FRANK MORLEY   *No.* 111

A voyage of six months in a ship, its one and only cabin
measuring 8 feet by 6 feet, up the Rhine, down the Danube,
passing from one to the other by the half-forgotten Ludwig's
Canal.

FAUSSET, Hugh l'Anson

TENNYSON. A critical study   *No.* 124

Mr. Fausset's study of Tennyson's qualities as poet, man and
moralist is by implication a study of some of the predominant
characteristics of the Victorian age. His book, however, is as
pictorial as it is critical, being woven, to quote *The Times*, 'like
an arras of delicate colour and imagery.'

FLAUBERT, Gustave

MADAME BOVARY. Translated by ELEANOR
MARX-AVELING. With an Introduction by HAMISH
MILES   *No.* 144

". . . It remains perpetually the novel of all novels which the
criticism of fiction cannot overlook; as soon as ever we speak
of the principles of the art we must be prepared to engage
with Flaubert. There is no such book as his *Bovary*; for
it is a novel in which the subject stands firm and clear, without the least shade of ambiguity to break the line which
bounds it.' PERCY LUBBOCK *in The Craft of Fiction*

FORMAN, Henry James

GRECIAN ITALY. A book of Travel   *No.* 29

'It has been said that if you were shown Taormina in a vision
you would not believe it. If the reader has been in Grecian
Italy before he reads this book, the magic of its pages will
revive old memories and induce a severe attack of nostalgia.'
From the Preface by H. FESTING JONES

FRASER, Ronald

THE FLYING DRAPER. A novel   *No.* 165

'After its own prodigal fashion the book rises as high above the
general run of novels as Codders did above the other drapers of
Primrose Hill.' *Punch*
'This is one of the very best first novels which we have seen since
the War, and its author, if he can maintain the standard which
he sets here, should go far.' *Daily Mail*

11

GARNETT, Edward

FRIDAY NIGHTS. Critical Essays   *No.* 119

'Mr. Garnett is "the critic as artist," sensitive alike to elemental nature and the subtlest human variations. His book sketches for us the possible outlines of a new humanism, a fresh valuation of both life and art.' *The Times*

GARNETT, Mrs. R. S.

THE INFAMOUS JOHN FRIEND. A Novel   *No.* 53

This book, though in form an historical novel, claims to rank as a psychological study. It is an attempt to depict a character which, though destitute of the common virtues of everyday life, is gifted with qualities that compel love and admiration.

GAUGIN, Paul

THE INTIMATE JOURNALS. Translated by VAN
WYCK BROOKS   *No.* 101

The confessions of genius are usually startling; and Gaugin's *Journals* are no exception. He exults in his power to give free rein to his savage spirit, tearing the shawl from convention's shoulders with a gesture as unscrupulous as it is Rabelaisian.

GIBBS, J. Arthur

A COTSWOLD VILLAGE   *No.* 138

'For pure observation of people, places and sports, occupations and wild life, the book is admirable. Everything is put down freshly from the notebook, and has not gone through any deadening process of being written up.' *Morning Post*

GOBINEAU, Le Comte de

THE CRIMSON HANDKERCHIEF AND OTHER
STORIES. Translated from the French by HENRY
LONGAN STUART   *No.* 137

The three stories included in this volume mark the flood tide of Comte de Gobineau's unique and long-neglected genius. Not even Nietzsche has surpassed him in a love of heroic characters and unfettered wills—or in his contempt for bourgeois virtues and vices.

GOSSE, Sir Edmund
SELECTED ESSAYS. First Series   *No. 73*

'The prose of Sir Edmund Gosse is as rich in the colour of young imagination as in the mellow harmony of judgment. Sir Edmund Gosse's literary kit-kats will continue to be read with avidity long after the greater part of the academic criticism of the century is swept away upon the lumber-heap.' *Daily Telegraph*

SELECTED ESSAYS. Second Series   *No. 81*

A second volume of essays personally chosen by Sir Edmund Gosse from the wide field of his literary work. One is delighted with the width of his appreciation which enables him to write with equal charm on *Wycherley* and on *How to Read the Bible*.

GRAHAM, Stephen
A PRIVATE IN THE GUARDS   *No. 89*

In his own experiences as a soldier Stephen Graham has conserved the half-forgotten emotions of a nation in arms. Above all, he makes us feel the stark brutality and horror of actual war, the valour which is more than valour.

HAMILTON, Mary Agnes
THOMAS CARLYLE   *No. 157*

Although not a formal biography, being more concerned with the mind of the man, as revealed in his writing, than with the external incidents of his life, it sets both Carlyle and Jane Welsh before the reader in an outline that is alive and challenging.

HASTINGS, A. C. G.
NIGERIAN DAYS. With an Introduction by R. B.
CUNNINGHAME GRAHAM   *No. 151*

Written with great sincerity and with equal modesty, it is the record of eighteen long years spent on the confines of the Empire, a book devoid of bombast, and without the cheap expression of opinion of the average globe-trotter.

HEARN, Lafcadio
GLEANINGS IN BUDDHA-FIELDS   *No. 42*

A book which is readable from the first page to the last, and is full of suggestive thought, the essays on Japanese religious belief calling for special praise for the earnest spirit in which the subject is approached.

13

HEARN, Lafcadio

GLIMPSES OF UNFAMILIAR JAPAN. First Series *No. 57*

Most books written about Japan have been superficial sketches of a passing traveller. Of the inner life of the Japanese we know practically nothing. Lafcadio Hearn reveals something of the people and their customs as they are.

GLIMPSES OF UNFAMILIAR JAPAN. Second Series *No. 58*

Sketches by an acute observer and a master of English prose, of a nation in transition—of the lingering remains of Old Japan, to-day only a memory, of its gardens, its beliefs, customs, gods and devils, of its wonderful kindliness and charm—and of the New Japan, struggling against odds towards new ideals.

KWAIDAN. Stories *No. 44*

The marvellous tales which Mr. Hearn has told in this volume illustrate the wonder-loving tendency of the Japanese. The stories are of goblins, fairies and sprites, with here and there an adventure into the field of unveiled supernaturalism.

OUT OF THE EAST *No. 43*

Mr. Hearn has written many books about Japan; he is saturated with the essence of its beauty, and in this book the light and colour and movement of that land drips from his pen in every delicately conceived and finely written sentence.

KOKORO *No. 172*

The heart, the inner meaning—that is the meaning of the Japanese word of the title. And it is the heart and inner meaning of Japan that Lafcadio Hearn recorded in the clear, musical prose of his essays.

HEMINGWAY, Ernest. Author of *A Farewell to Arms*

MEN WITHOUT WOMEN. Stories *No. 159*

'Mr. Hemingway has the art of making what he describes take place before our eyes, as if we saw it upon the stage. Brilliant is not a brilliant enough word for it.' *Daily News*

HEYWARD, Du Bose

PORGY. A Tale *No. 85*

This fascinating book gives a vivid and intimate insight into the lives of a group of American negroes, from whom Porgy stands out, rich in humour and tragedy.

HILDEBRAND, Arthur Sturges

BLUE WATER. The story of an ocean voyage. With
an Introductory Memoir by HARRISON SMITH   *No. 36*
> This book gives the real feeling of life on a small cruising yacht;
> the nights on deck with the sails against the sky, long fights with
> head winds by mountainous coasts to safety in forlorn little
> island ports, and constant adventure free from care.

HINDUS, Maurice

BROKEN EARTH   *No. 174*
> This is a very human book. It deals with one of the most
> exciting periods in the history of the Russian village—a period
> of universal heart-searching with peasants as ever giving free
> vent to their thoughts and troubles. Like *Red Bread*, the scene
> of *Broken Earth* is laid in the author's native village.

HOULT, Norah

POOR WOMEN   *No. 168*
> 'I know of nothing written in late years with which to compare
> them. They are the unique manifestations which genius always
> gives us. Norah Hoult's gift for narrative is the right magic for
> story telling.' H. M. TOMLINSON

HOUSMAN, Laurence

ANGELS AND MINISTERS, AND OTHER
PLAYS. Imaginary portraits of political characters
done in dialogue—Queen Victoria, Disraeli, Gladstone,
Parnell, Joseph Chamberlain and Woodrow Wilson   *No. 17*
> 'It is all so good that one is tempted to congratulate Mr. Housman
> on a true masterpiece.' *Times.*

HUDDLESTON, Sisley

FRANCE AND THE FRENCH. A study   *No. 86*
> 'His book is a repository of facts marshalled with judgment; as
> such it should assist in clearing away a whole maze of mis-
> conceptions and prejudices, and serve as a sort of pocket
> encyclopædia of modern France.' *Times Literary Supplement*

HUDSON, W. H.

MEN, BOOKS AND BIRDS: Letters to a Friend.
With Notes, some Letters, and an Introduction by
MORLEY ROBERTS   *No. 112*
> An important collection of letters from the naturalist to his
> friend, literary executor and fellow author, Morley Roberts,
> covering a period of twenty-five years.

JEWETT, Sarah Orne

THE COUNTRY OF THE POINTED FIRS. Stories *No. 28*

'The young student of American literature in the far distant future will take up this book and say "a masterpiece!" as proudly as if he had made it. It will be a message in a universal language—the one message that even the scythe of Time spares.' *From the Preface by* WILLA CATHER

JOHNSON, Samuel

A JOURNEY TO THE WESTERN ISLANDS OF SCOTLAND. With a foreword by D. L. MURRAY *No. 162*

'To Scotland however he ventured; and he returned from it in great good humour, with his prejudices much lessened, and with very grateful feelings of the hospitality with which he was treated; as is evident from that admirable work his *Journey to the Western Islands of Scotland*.' BOSWELL

JONES, Henry Festing

DIVERSIONS IN SICILY. Travel impressions *No. 120*

Shortly before his death, Mr. Festing Jones chose out *Diversions in Sicily* for reprinting from among his three books of mainly Sicilian sketches and studies. These chapters, as well as any that he wrote, recapture the wisdom, charm and humour of their author.

JOYCE, James

DUBLINERS. A volume of Stories *No. 14*

A collection of fifteen short stories by the author of *Ulysses*. They are all of them brave, relentless and sympathetic pictures of Dublin life; realistic, perhaps, but not crude; analytical, but not repugnant.

A PORTRAIT OF THE ARTIST AS A YOUNG MAN. A novel *No. 155*

'It is a book to buy and read. Its claim to be literature is as good as the claim of the last book of *Gulliver's Travels*. It is by far the most living and convincing picture that exists of an Irish Catholic upbringing. The technique is startling. . . . A most memorable novel.' H. G. WELLS

KALLAS, Aino

THE WHITE SHIP. Stories. With an Introduction
by JOHN GALSWORTHY   *No.* 24

'The writer has an extraordinary sense of atmosphere.' *Times Literary Supplement*

'Stories told convincingly and well, with a keen perception for natural beauty.' *Nation*

KOMROFF, Manuel

CONTEMPORARIES OF MARCO POLO   *No.* 123

This volume comprises the Travel Records in the Eastern parts of the world of William of Rubruck (1253–5), the Journey of John of Pian de Carpini (1245–7), the Journey of Friar Odoric (1318–30). They describe the marvels and wonders of Asia under the Khans.

THE TRAVELS OF MARCO POLO   *No.* 59

When Marco Polo arrived at the court of the Great Khan Pekin had just been rebuilt. Kublai Khan was at the height of his glory. Polo rose rapidly in favour and became governor of an important district. In this way he gained first-hand knowledge of a great civilisation and described it with astounding accuracy and detail.

LAWRENCE, A. W., edited by

CAPTIVES OF TIPU. Survivors' Narratives   *No.* 125

In addition to the well-known stories of Bristow and Scurry, a soldier and a seaman, who were forcibly Mohammedanised and retained in the service of Mysore till their escape after ten years, extracts are given from an officer's diary of his close imprisonment at Seringapatam.

THE WRECK OF THE *MEDUSA*. The Narratives
of Dard, Corréard and Savigny   *No.* 163

In 1816 a French warship ran aground upon an African reef. There was no immediate danger, yet mismanagement and aimless panic developed a series of savageries perhaps unequalled in men of this civilisation. After the desertion of comrades and the wanton destruction of food and drink, follow suicide, murder and cannibalism, mutiny and calculated massacre, on a half-submerged and broken raft.

LAWRENCE, D. H.
TWILIGHT IN ITALY. Travel essays   *No.* 19
This volume of travel vignettes in North Italy was first published in 1916. In *Twilight in Italy* will be found all the freshness and vigour of outlook which made the author a force in literature.

LAWSON, Henry
WHILE THE BILLY BOILS. First Series   *No.* 38
These stories are written by the O. Henry of Australia. They tell of men and dogs, of cities and plains, of gullies and ridges of sorrow and happiness, and of the fundamental goodness that is hidden in the most unpromising of human soil.

WHILE THE BILLY BOILS. Second Series   *No.* 39
Mr. Lawson has the uncanny knack of making the people he writes about almost violently alive. Whether he tells of jackeroos, bush children or drovers' wives, each one lingers in the memory long after we have closed the book.

LESLIE, Shane
THE END OF A CHAPTER   *No.* 110
In this, his most famous book, Mr. Shane Leslie has preserved for future generations the essence of the pre-war epoch, its institutions and individuals. He writes of Eton, of the Empire, of Post-Victorianism, of the Politicians. . . . And whatever he touches upon, he brilliantly interprets.

LINKLATER, Eric
WHITE-MAA'S SAGA   *No.* 180
'Mr. Linklater has a way with him. He has wit and insight and an unfamiliar background to help him. . . . What he has done, and done remarkably well, is to tell the plain tale of a young man from Orkney who, after fighting in France, tries to become a doctor, fails, and finds something like happiness in another direction.' *Sunday Times*

LITHGOW, William
RARE ADVENTURES AND PAINEFULL PEREGRINATIONS (1582-1645). Edited and
with Introduction by B. I. LAWRENCE   *No.* 109
This is a book of a seventeenth-century Scotchman who walked over the Levant, North Africa and most of Europe, including Spain, where he was tortured by the Inquisition. An unscrupulous man, full of curiosity, his comments are diverting and penetrating, his adventures remarkable.

LUBBOCK, Percy

EARLHAM. A portrait *No. 6*

'The book seems too intimate to be reviewed. We want to be allowed to read it, and to dream over it, and keep silence about it. His judgment is perfect, his humour is true and ready; his touch light and prim; his prose is exact and clean and full of music.' *Times*

ROMAN PICTURES. Studies *No. 21*

Pictures of life as it is lived—or has been or might be lived— among the pilgrims and colonists in Rome of more or less English speech. 'A book of whimsical originality and exquisite workmanship, and worthy of one of the best prose writers of our time.' *Sunday Times*

THE CRAFT OF FICTION. Critical essays *No. 5*

'No more substantial or more charming volume of criticism has been published in our time.' *Observer*
'To say that this is the best book on the subject is probably true; but it is more to the point to say that it is the only one.' *Times Literary Supplement*

LYND, Robert

BOOKS AND AUTHORS. Critical essays *No. 135*

Among the modern writers we have appreciations of Mr. Max Beerbohm, Mr. Arnold Bennett and Mr. H. M. Tomlinson, while Herrick, Keats, Charles Lamb and Hawthorne are a few of the classical writers who are criticised in the book.

MACDONALD, The Rt. Hon. J. Ramsay

WANDERINGS AND EXCURSIONS. Essays *No. 132*

Mr. Ramsay MacDonald has been a wide traveller and reader, and has an uncommon power of bringing an individual eye— the eye of the artist—to bear upon whatever he sees.

MACHEN, Arthur

DOG AND DUCK. Essays *No. 15*

'As a literary artist, Mr. Arthur Machen has few living equals, and that is very far indeed from being his only, or even his greatest, claim on the suffrages of English readers.' *Sunday Times*

MASEFIELD, John

CAPTAIN MARGARET. A Novel   *No.* 35

'His style is crisp, curt and vigorous. He has the Stevensonian sea-swagger, the Stevensonian sense of beauty and poetic spirit. Mr. Masefield's descriptions ring true and his characters carry conviction.' *The Observer*

MASON, Arthur

THE FLYING BO'SUN. A Tale   *No.* 47

'What makes the book remarkable is the imaginative power which has re-created these events so vividly that even the supernatural ones come with the shock and the conviction with which actual supernatural events might come.' *From the Introduction by* EDWIN MUIR

WIDE SEAS AND MANY LANDS. Reminiscences

With an Introduction by MAURICE BARING   *No.* 7

'This is an extremely entertaining, and at the same time moving, book. We are in the presence of a born writer. We read with the same mixture of amazement and delight that fills us throughout a Conrad novel.' *New Statesman*

MAUGHAM, W. Somerset

LIZA OF LAMBETH. A Tale   *No.* 141

Liza of Lambeth is Mr. Somerset Maugham's first novel, and its publication decided the whole course of his life. For if it had not succeeded its author could not have turned from medicine to letters. The story reflects much of the experience which Mr. Maugham gathered when he worked in the slums of the East End as a doctor.

ON A CHINESE SCREEN. Sketches   *No.* 31

A collection of sketches of life in China. Mr. Somerset Maugham writes with equal certainty and vigour whether his characters are Chinese or European.

THE CASUARINA TREE. Stories   *No.* 92

Intensely dramatic stories in which the stain of the East falls deeply on the lives of English men and women. On passion and its culminating tragedy he looks with unmoved detachment, ringing the changes without comment and yet with little cynicism.

MAUGHAM, W. Somerset

THE MOON AND SIXPENCE. A Novel   *No.* 91

'Mr. Maugham has given us a ruthless and penetrating study in personality with a savage truthfulness of delineation and an icy contempt for the heroic and the sentimental.' *The Times*

THE GENTLEMAN IN THE PARLOUR   *No.* 179

'Mr. Maugham recently travelled from Rangoon by river to Mandalay, on horseback through the mountains and forests of the Shan States to Bangkok and by sea to Haiphong. Result: *The Gentleman in the Parlour*, a desultory sketch book, very little descriptive of the conventional "sights" but occupied, to our richer delight, with personal encounters and reflections by the way. These are the things that give every journey unique value; but only the artist is sufficiently aware of that to shed the rest and keep only them.' HORACE THOROGOOD in the *Evening Standard*

MENCKEN, H. L.

IN DEFENCE OF WOMEN   *No.* 50

'All I design by the book is to set down in more or less plain form certain ideas that practically every civilised man and woman hold *in petto*, but that have been concealed hitherto by the vast mass of sentimentalities swathing the whole woman question.' *From the Author's Introduction*

SELECTED PREJUDICES. First Series. A Book of Essays.   *No.* 8

'He is exactly the kind of man we are needing, an iconoclast, a scoffer at ideals, a critic with whips and scorpions who does not hesitate to deal with literary, social and political humbug in the one slashing fashion.' *English Review*

SELECTED PREJUDICES. Second Series   *No.* 60

'What a master of the straight left in appreciation! Everybody who wishes to see how common sense about books and authors can be made exhilarating should acquire this delightful book.' *Morning Post*

MEREZHKOVSKY, Dmitri

DECEMBER THE FOURTEENTH. A Novel
Translated from the Russian by NATALIE DUDDINGTON
With an Introduction by MARY AGNES HAMILTON   *No.* 156

> 'It lives on its own account, and is as wildly exciting as the story of a conspiracy can be, but it has certain universal qualities. It becomes as you read, not simply an historically accurate picture of a particular revolt, but a picture of all resistance to all tyrants throughout the ages.' DAVID GARNETT

MEYNELL, Alice

WAYFARING. Essays   *No.* 133

> 'Her essays have the merit of saying just enough of the subject, and they can be read repeatedly. The surprise coming from that combined grace of manner and sanity of thought is like one's dream of what the recognition of a new truth would be.' Some of the essays so described by George Meredith are here collected in book-form for the first time.

MILES, Hamish

SELECTIONS FROM BYRON. Poetry and Prose   *No.* 154

> Byron's poetry, the core of his legend and so often the mirror of his life, is too often left unread. This selection, which includes some examples of his prose, is designed to show not only how his verse reflects the drama of Byron's own life, but also how brilliantly Byron diagnosed the evils of the post-war era in which his stirring life was spent.

MITCHISON, Naomi

CLOUD CUCKOO LAND. A Novel of Sparta   *No.* 88

> 'Rich and frank in passions, and rich, too, in the detail which helps to make feigned life seem real.' *Times Literary Supplement*

THE CONQUERED. A story of the Gauls under Cæsar *No.* 45

> 'With *The Conquered* Mrs. Mitchison establishes herself as the best, if not the only, English historical novelist now writing. It seems to me in many respects the most attractive and poignant historical novel I have ever read.' *New Statesman*

MITCHISON, Naomi

WHEN THE BOUGH BREAKS. Stories of the time
when Rome was crumbling to ruin *No. 46*

'Interesting, delightful and fresh as morning dew. The con-
noisseur in short stories will turn to some pages in this volume
again and again with renewed relish.' *Times Literary Supplement*

BLACK SPARTA. Stories of Sparta and Athens *No. 158*

'Her touch is sure, her description admirable. The reader gets
a whiff of crushed thyme and of dew on dust as the author tells
of Pindar's poetic adventure into Thessaly.' *Times*

MONTAGU, Lady Mary Wortley

THE TRAVEL LETTERS OF LADY MARY
WORTLEY MONTAGU. Edited by A. W.
LAWRENCE *No. 143*

In the words of Tobias Smollett: 'These *Letters* will show, as
long as the English language endures, the sprightliness of her
wit, the solidity of her judgment, the elegance of her taste, and
the excellence of her real character. They are so bewitchingly
entertaining, that we defy the most phlegmatic man on earth
to read one without going through with them.'

MOORE, George

CONFESSIONS OF A YOUNG MAN *No. 76*

'Mr. Moore, true to his period and to his genius, stripped himself of everything that might stand between him and the
achievement of his artistic object. He does not ask you to
admire this George Moore. He merely asks you to observe
him beyond good and evil as a constant plucked from the
bewildering flow of eternity.' HUMBERT WOLFE

MORAND, Paul

OPEN ALL NIGHT *No. 175*

Six sketches in post-war feminine psychology. M. Morand's
young ladies, whether of Barcelona or Constantinople, Rome or
Paris, Buda Pesth or Scandinavia, are all well worth meeting—
in print.

'The most interesting book by a young French author we
have seen for many months.' J. MIDDLETON MURRY in the
Nation

'I must regard this book as a great literary event and a great
literary guide in the darkness of present-day Europe.' T. P.
O'CONNOR in *Cassell's Weekly*

23

MORAND, Paul

CLOSED ALL NIGHT   *No.* 176

The masculine pendant to *Open All Night*, showing the postwar man in Dublin, in Berlin, in Paris and in London. An Irish poet turned politician, an ex-officer of the Prussian Guard, and a Syrian who mends the complexions and repairs the bodies of London ladies; these and others appear in M. Morand's lively pages.

'It is a sign of the times that M. Morand should be so naturally included with the immortals, but no one who has revelled in his peculiar talent would deny him that privilege.' *Times*

MORLEY, Christopher

SAFETY PINS. Essays. With an Introduction by
H. M. TOMLINSON   *No.* 98

Mr. Morley is an author who is content to move among his fellows, to note, to reflect, and to write genially and urbanely; to love words for their sound as well as for their value in expression of thought.

THUNDER ON THE LEFT. A Novel   *No.* 90

'It is personal to every reader, it will become for every one a reflection of himself. I fancy that here, as always where work is fine and true, the author has created something not as he would but as he must, and is here an interpreter of a world more wonderful than he himself knows.' HUGH WALPOLE

WHERE THE BLUE BEGINS. A Fantasy   *No.* 74

'Mr. Morley is a master of consequent inconsequence. His humour and irony are excellent, and his satire is only the more salient for the delicate and ingenuous fantasy in which it is set.' *Manchester Guardian*

MURRAY, D. L.

CANDLES AND CRINOLINES. Essays   *No.* 149

Mr. Murray's sub-acid Tory satisfaction enlivens the historical essays, his sanity and penetration make memorable the books he discusses, while the unfailing charm of his style suffuses the reader of his miscellaneous pieces with mood and sentiment such as might be evolved from the glow of candles upon crinolines.

MURRAY, Max

THE WORLD'S BACK DOORS. Adventures. With
an Introduction by HECTOR BOLITHO   *No.* 61

His journey round the world was begun with about enough
money to buy one meal, and continued for 66,000 miles. There
are periods as a longshoreman and as a sailor, and a Chinese
guard and a night watchman, and as a hobo.

MURRY, J. Middleton

THE EVOLUTION OF AN INTELLECTUAL   *No.* 62

These essays were written during and immediately after the
Great War. The author says that they record the painful stages
by which he passed from the so-called intellectual state to the
state of being what he now considers to be a reasonable man.

DISCOVERIES   *No.* 152

These essays are an attempt to make plain some of the underlying motives of great literature. Shakespeare holds the chief
place in the book. In the essays on *Tchekov* and *Russian Literature*; on *Herman Melville* and *American Poetry*; on *Marcel
Proust*—the same fundamental pre-occupation, to discover
la vraie vie, is shown at work.

NICHOLS, Beverley

TWENTY-FIVE. An Autobiography   *No.* 147

'I have read every word of it. It has life and good nature. It is
full of fun—written with an easy, vivid English.' SOMERSET
MAUGHAM in *The Sunday Times*

O'FLAHERTY, Liam

SPRING SOWING. Stories   *No.* 26

'Nothing seems to escape Mr. O'Flaherty's eye; his brain turns
all things to drama; and his vocabulary is like a river in spate.
Spring Sowing is a book to buy, or to borrow, or, yes, to steal.'
Bookman

THE BLACK SOUL. A Novel   *No.* 99

'*The Black Soul* overwhelms one like a storm. . . . Nothing
like it has been written by any Irish writer.' 'Æ' in *The Irish
Statesman*

O'FLAHERTY, Liam
THE INFORMER. A Novel *No.* 128
This realistic novel of the Dublin underworld is generally conceded to be Mr. O'Flaherty's most outstanding book. It is to be produced as a film by British International Pictures, who regard it as one of the most ambitious of their efforts.

O'NEILL, Eugene
THE MOON OF THE CARIBBEES, AND OTHER PLAYS OF THE SEA. With an Introduction by
ST. JOHN ERVINE *No.* 116
'Mr. O'Neill is immeasurably the most interesting man of letters that America has produced since the death of Walt Whitman.'
From the Introduction

O'SHAUGHNESSY, Edith
VIENNESE MEDLEY. A Novel *No.* 51
'It is told with infinite tenderness, with many touches of grave or poignant humour, in a very beautiful book, which no lover of fiction should allow to pass unread. A book which sets its writer definitely in the first rank of living English novelists.'
Sunday Times

PATER, Walter
MARIUS THE EPICUREAN *No.* 23
Walter Pater was at the same time a scholar of wide sympathies and a master of the English language. He describes with rare delicacy of feeling and insight the religious and philosophic tendencies of the Roman Empire at the time of Antoninus Pius as they affected the mind and life of the story's hero.

THE RENAISSANCE *No.* 63
This English classic contains studies of those 'supreme artists' Michelangelo and Da Vinci, and of Botticelli, Della Robia, Mirandola, and others, who 'have a distinct faculty of their own by which they convey to us a peculiar quality of pleasure which we cannot get elsewhere.'

PICKTHALL, Marmaduke
ORIENTAL ENCOUNTERS *No.* 103
In *Oriental Encounters*, Mr. Pickthall relives his earlier manhood's discovery of Arabia and sympathetic encounters with the Eastern mind. He is one of the few travellers who really bridges the racial gulf.

26

POWELL, Sydney Walter
THE ADVENTURES OF A WANDERER   *No.* 64

Throwing up a position in the Civil Service in Natal because he preferred movement and freedom to monotony and security, the author started his wanderings by enlisting in an Indian Ambulance Corps in the South African War. Afterwards he wandered all over the world.

POWYS, Llewelyn
BLACK LAUGHTER   *No.* 127

Black Laughter is a kind of *Robinson Crusoe* of the continent of Africa. You actually share the sensations of a sensitive and artistic nature suddenly transplanted from a peaceful English village into the heart of Africa.

PROWSE, R. O.
A GIFT OF THE DUSK. With an Introduction by
J. MIDDLETON MURRY   *No.* 178

The scene is a retreat among Swiss mountains, a place of sunlight and a place of exile, the life of which is depicted as it is really lived beneath the blinds of the sunlit balconies. It is the story of two people who, in a companionship intimate as their loneliness, poignant as their need, discover the gift that the dusk of their lives has to give.

RANSOME, Arthur
RACUNDRA'S FIRST CRUISE   *No.* 65

'His experiences and adventures in fair and dirty weather, the places he visited, the primitive life of the Esthonian islanders, some extraordinarily beautiful anecdotes, and the charm and humour of Mr. Ransome's writing, form a book of which there is little more to be said than that it is delightful—a pleasure to read from beginning to end.' *The Spectator*

READE, Winwood
THE MARTYRDOM OF MAN   *No.* 66

'Few sketches of universal history by one single author have been written. One book that has influenced me very strongly is *The Martyrdom of Man*. This "dates," as people say nowadays, and it has a fine gloom of its own; but it is still an extraordinarily inspiring presentation of human history as one consistent process.' H. G. WELLS in *An Outline of History*

REYNOLDS, Stephen

A POOR MAN'S HOUSE   *No.* 93

Vivid and intimate pictures of a Devonshire fisherman's life.
'Compact, harmonious, without a single—I won't say false—
but uncertain note, true in aim, sentiment and expression, precise and imaginative, never precious, but containing here and
there an absolutely priceless phrase. . . .' JOSEPH CONRAD

RIESENBERG, Felix

SHIPMATES. Seafaring portraits   *No.* 107

A collection of intimate character-portraits of men with whom
the author has sailed on many voyages. The sequence of studies
blends into a fascinating panorama of living characters.

ROBERTS, Captain George

A SERIES OF UNCOMMON EVENTS   *No.* 40

The Manner of his being taken by Three Pyrate Ships which,
after having plundered him, and detained him 10 Days, put
him aboard his own Sloop, without Provisions, Water, etc.
The Hardships he endur'd for above 20 Days, 'till he arriv'd at
the Island of St. Nicholas, from whence he was blown off to Sea;
and after Four Days of Difficulty and Distress, was Ship-
wreck'd on the Unfrequented Island of St. John.

ROBINSON, James Harvey

THE MIND IN THE MAKING. An Essay   *No.* 9

'For me, I think James Harvey Robinson is going to be almost
as important as was Huxley in my adolescence, and William
James in later years. It is a cardinal book. I question whether
in the long run people may not come to it, as making a new
initiative into the world's thoughts and methods.' *From the
Introduction by* H. G. WELLS

ROSEBERY, The Earl of

NAPOLEON : THE LAST PHASE   *No.* 96

Of books and memoirs about Napoleon there is indeed no end,
but of the veracious books such as this there are remarkably few.
It aims to penetrate the deliberate darkness which surrounds the
last act of the Napoleonic drama.

RUTHERFORD, Mark

THE AUTOBIOGRAPHY OF MARK RUTHER-
FORD. With an Introduction by H. W. MASSINGHAM   *No. 67*

Because of its honesty, delicacy and simplicity of portraiture, this book has always had a curious grip upon the affections of its readers. An English Amiel, inheriting to his comfort an English Old Crome landscape, he freed and strengthened his own spirit as he will his reader's.

THE DELIVERANCE   *No. 68*

Once read, Hale White [Mark Rutherford] is never forgotten. But he is not yet approached through the highways of English letters. To the lover of his work, nothing can be more attractive than the pure and serene atmosphere of thought in which his art moves.

THE REVOLUTION IN TANNER'S LANE   *No. 69*

'Since Bunyan, English Puritanism has produced one imaginative genius of the highest order. To my mind, our fiction contains no more perfectly drawn pictures of English life in its recurring emotional contrast of excitement and repose more valuable to the historian, or more stimulating to the imaginative reader.' H. W. MASSINGHAM

SHELVOCKE, Captain George

A PRIVATEER'S VOYAGE ROUND THE
WORLD. With aspersions upon him by WILLIAM
BETAGH. Edited by A. W. LAWRENCE   *No. 142*

A book of 1726, well known as the source of the albatross incident and other passages in the 'Ancient Mariner'; it describes the exploits of a private ship of war on the coasts of South America, its wreck on the Crusoe island of Juan Fernandez, and the subsequent adventures of its company in various parts of the Pacific.

SITWELL, Constance

FLOWERS AND ELEPHANTS. With an Intro-
duction by E. M. FORSTER   *No. 115*

Mrs. Sitwell has known India well, and has filled her pages with many vivid little pictures, and with sounds and scents. But it is the thread on which her impressions are strung that is so fascinating, a thread so delicate and rare that the slightest clumsiness in definition would snap it.

SMITH, Pauline

THE BEADLE. A Novel of South Africa *No.* 129

'A story of great beauty, and told with simplicity and tenderness that makes it linger in the memory. It is a notable contribution to the literature of the day.' *Morning Post*

THE LITTLE KAROO. Stories of South Africa
With an Introduction by ARNOLD BENNETT *No.* 104

'Nothing like this has been written about South African life since Olive Schreiner and her *Story of an African Farm* took the literary world by storm.' *The Daily Telegraph*

SQUIRE, J. C.

THE GRUB STREET NIGHTS ENTERTAINMENTS *No.* 102

Stories of literary life, told with a breath of fantasy and gaily ironic humour. Each character lives, and is the more lively for its touch of caricature.

SULLIVAN, J. W. N.

ASPECTS OF SCIENCE. First Series *No.* 70

Although they deal with different aspects of various scientific ideas the papers which make up this volume do illustrate, more or less, one point of view. This book tries to show one or two of the many reasons why science may be interesting for people who are not specialists as well as for those who are.

SYMONS, Arthur

PLAYS, ACTING AND MUSIC *No.* 113

This book deals mainly with music and with the various arts of the stage. Mr. Arthur Symons shows how each art has its own laws, its own limits; these it is the business of the critic jealously to distinguish. Yet in the study of art as art it should be his endeavour to master the universal science of beauty.

WILLIAM BLAKE. A critical study *No.* 94

When Blake spoke the first word of the nineteenth century there was none to hear it; and now that his message has penetrated the world, and is slowly remaking it, few are conscious of the man who first voiced it. This lack of knowledge is remedied in Mr. Symons's work.

TCHEKOFF, Anton

TWO PLAYS: *The Cherry Orchard* and *The Sea Gull.*

Translated by GEORGE CALDERON   *No.* 33

Tchekoff had that fine comedic spirit which relishes the incongruity between the actual disorder of the world with the underlying order. He habitually mingled tragedy (which is life seen close at hand) with comedy (which is life seen at a distance). His plays are tragedies with the texture of comedy.

THOMAS, Edward

A LITERARY PILGRIM IN ENGLAND   *No.* 95

A book about the homes and resorts of English writers, from John Aubrey, Cowper, Gilbert White, Cobbett, Wordsworth, Burns, Borrow and Lamb, to Swinburne, Stevenson, Meredith, W. H. Hudson and H. Belloc.

THE POCKET BOOK OF POEMS AND SONGS FOR THE OPEN AIR   *No.* 97

This anthology is meant to please those lovers of poetry and the country who like a book that can always lighten some of their burdens or give wings to their delight, whether in the open air by day, or under the roof at evening; in it is gathered much of the finest English poetry.

TURGENEV, Ivan

FATHERS AND CHILDREN. Translated by CONSTANCE GARNETT   *No.* 83

'As a piece of art, *Fathers and Children* is the most powerful of all Turgenev's works. The figure of Bazarov is not only the political centre of the book, but a figure in which the eternal tragedy of man's impotence and insignificance is realised in scenes of a most ironical human drama.' EDWARD GARNETT

ON THE EVE. Translated by CONSTANCE GARNETT   *No.* 82

On the Eve is a quiet work, yet over which the growing consciousness of coming events casts its heavy shadow. Turgenev, even as he sketched the ripening love of a young girl, has made us feel the dawning aspirations of a nation.

SMOKE. Translated by CONSTANCE GARNETT   *No.* 84

In this novel Turgenev sees and reflects, even in the shifting phases of political life, that which is universal in human nature. His work is compassionate, beautiful, unique; in the sight of his fellow-craftsmen always marvellous and often perfect.

VERGA, Giovanni

MASTRO-DON GESUALDO. A Novel. Translated by D. H. LAWRENCE   No. 71

Verga, who died in 1922, is recognised as one of the greatest of Italian writers of fiction. 'It is a fine full tale, a fine full picture of life, with a bold beauty of its own which Mr. Lawrence must have relished greatly as he translated it.' *Observer*

CAVALLERIA RUSTICANA   No. 173

Giovanni Verga, a Sicilian, died in 1922. His work is of the blood and salt of Sicily. Practically all serious Italian critics regard Verga as the greatest of Italian writers of fiction with the single exception of Manzoni. As far as style goes, Verga aims to be unliterary, to be close to the spoken language of his characters. The story is the original upon which Mascagni's opera was written.

VOIGT, F. A.

COMBED OUT   No. 122

This account of life in the army in 1917–18, both at home and in France, is written with a telling incisiveness. The author does not indulge in an unnecessary word, but packs in just the right details with an intensity of feeling that is infectious.

WATERS, W. G.

TRAVELLER'S JOY. An Anthology   No. 106

This anthology has been selected for publication in the Travellers' Library from among the many collections of verse because of its suitability for the traveller, particularly the summer and autumn traveller, who would like to carry with him some store of literary provender.

WELLS, H. G.

CHRISTINA ALBERTA'S FATHER. A Novel.   No. 100

'At first reading the book is utterly beyond criticism ; all the characters are delightfully genuine.' *Spectator*
'Brimming over with Wellsian insight, humour and invention. No one but Mr. Wells could have written the whole book and given it such a verve and sparkle.' *Westminster Gazette*

WELLS, H. G.

THE DREAM. A Novel   *No.* 20

'It is the richest, most generous and absorbing thing that Mr. Wells has given us for years and years.' *Daily News*

'I find this book as close to being magnificent as any book that I have ever read. It is full of inspiration and life.' *Daily Graphic*

WHARTON, Edith

IN MOROCCO   *No.* 41

Morocco is a land of mists and mysteries, of trailing silver veils through which minarets, mighty towers, hot palm groves and Atlas snows peer and disappear at the will of the Atlantic cloud-drifts.

ITALIAN BACKGROUNDS   *No.* 114

Mrs. Wharton's perception of beauty and her grace of writing are matters of general acceptance. Her book gives us pictures of mountains and rivers, monks, nuns and saints.

WHITAKER, Malachi

FROST IN APRIL   *No.* 181

'This collection of short stories, impressions, incidents and mere notes about life has a number of things to recommend it—variety, sincerity, a feeling for beauty and a sort of eagerness that is refreshing.' *Times Literary Supplement*

WITHERS, Percy

FRIENDS IN SOLITUDE. With an Introduction by
LASCELLES ABERCROMBIE   *No.* 131

Percy Withers, who lived for many years in the Lake Country, selects certain of the dale folk to tell in their own fashion so much the manner of men they are, so much of their life-story, of its prosperities, endurances, pathos, as may make the picture of his own experience more complete and give to it a more human significance.

ZANGWILL, Israel

THE KING OF SCHNORRERS   *No.* 164

Humour of a rich and active character pervades the delightful history of Menhasseh, the magnificently autocratic king of Schnorrers, or Jewish beggars, who, dressed in his dirty rags, was as haughty in demanding charity as in accepting it.

The Life and Letters Series has been reviewed by Mr. Frank Swinnerton in *The Evening News* thus:

'The first volumes of this new and handsome series should meet the most modern taste. Here in beautiful light form are books which have all been previously published within the last three or four years at much higher prices.

'Of the first titles every one is the kind of work to make any keen reader say to himself, "I wish I could afford that! If it were cheaper I'd buy it!"

'With the price 4s. 6d. a volume, the appearance handsome and very agreeable, *The Life and Letters Series* CAN be afforded. The bargain will be a good one.'

ANTHONY, Katharine
CATHERINE THE GREAT. With a Frontispiece   *No.* 13
'This lively and well-written study is a judicious treatment of a temperament and a reputation, and the whole book is a contribution to the study, not only of Catherine the Great, but of a significant period in Russian history.' *Time and Tide*

BELLOC, Hilaire
A CONVERSATION WITH AN ANGEL   *No.* 27
In this volume of essays Mr. Belloc well maintains his usual high level of pungent and witty writing. His subjects are varied as they are diverting, and include pages on poverty, academic hate and epigrams, on Renan, Gibbon and Macaulay, on witchcraft, pavement artists and bridges.

BERCOVICI, Konrad
THE STORY OF THE GYPSIES. Illustrated from
photographs by E. O. HOPPÉ   *No.* 11
'The author of this fascinating book has not only made researches into the history of this people but has also lived, travelled and been entertained by them. Though it would be extravagant to say that he had the genius of George Borrow, it is certain that he has more respect for the truth and for scholarly fact than had that great though erratic man.' *Listener*

BIRKENHEAD, The late Earl of, edited by
THE ADVENTURES OF RALPH RASHLEIGH
(a penal exile in Australia 1825-1844). Illustrated from
facsimile pages of the original MS.   *No.* 20
> This book reveals, through the sufferings and vicissitudes of a
> single convict transported to New South Wales for burglary, a
> vivid picture of the conditions under which the penal code was
> administered less than a hundred years ago.

BONE, James
THE LONDON PERAMBULATOR.   Illustrated
with drawings by MUIRHEAD BONE   *No.* 23
> 'The quiet humour of the writer and hand of the artist go
> together to present the majesty, the beauty, the variety, the
> oddity of London in a book one would not soon tire of
> praising.' *Times Literary Supplement*

BROWNLEE, Frank
CATTLE THIEF   *No.* 32
> This is the life story of a South African native. In its divination
> of the native mind the book is a little masterpiece. More than
> this, the exploits of Ntsukumbini, a member of a family of
> professional stock thieves, his outwitting of the police, his
> experiences in the gold mines, his loves and sorrows, make
> really good reading.

BUTLER, Samuel
EREWHON. A Satire. Illustrated with woodcuts by
ROBERT GIBBINGS   *No.* 16
> 'To lash the age, to ridicule vain pretensions, to expose
> hypocrisy, to deride humbug in education, politics and religion,
> are tasks beyond most men's powers ; but occasionally, very
> occasionally, a bit of genuine satire secures for itself more than
> a passing nod of recognition. *Erewhon* is such a satire. . . .
> The best of its kind since *Gulliver's Travels.*' AUGUSTINE
> BIRRELL

ALPS AND SANCTUARIES. Illustrated with two
maps   *No.* 25
> '*Alps and Sanctuaries* is essentially a holiday book, and no one
> ever enjoyed a holiday more keenly than Butler. Here we
> see him in his most unbuttoned mood, giving the rein to his
> high spirits and letting his fantastic humour carry him
> whither it would.' *From the Introduction by* R. A. STREATFEILD

CUMMINGS, E. E.

THE ENORMOUS ROOM. With a Frontispiece
portrait of the Author, and an Introduction by
ROBERT GRAVES   *No.* 2

'He reveals himself as a man of sensibility and fortitude, and
he writes always with such good taste that I do not think anyone reading his book, could feel otherwise than that it is the
work of a rare, fine spirit.' *Sunday Times*

DARK, Sidney

FIVE DEANS. With five illustrations   *No.* 26

'The five Deans drawn and characterised in this book are
Colet, Donne, Swift, Stanley, and Inge. . . . It is extraordinarily brilliant, carrying the reader on with unflagging
interest from beginning to end. The writer is gifted with a
sure instinctive capacity to exclude the dull and the heavy, and
to include the humanly interesting and attractive.' *The Church
Times*

DAVIES, W. H.

THE AUTOBIOGRAPHY OF A SUPER-TRAMP.
Illustrated from four portraits of the Author and an
Introduction by GEORGE BERNARD SHAW   *No.* 6

'I recommend this most remarkable Autobiography of a
Super-Tramp to your special attention.' GEORGE BERNARD
SHAW

DE KRUIF, Paul

MICROBE HUNTERS. Illustrated by four portraits *No.* 3

This book captures for the reader something of the intellectual
excitement and romance associated with the works of the
greater scientists.

DIMNET, Ernest

THE BRONTË SISTERS. With four Illustrations   *No.* 19

The Brontë Sisters is an ideal co-mingling of critical biography
and literary criticism. With great tenderness, with much sympathy, but with rigid intellectual honesty, the author recreates
for us the parsonage and its inhabitants, and brings especially to
the mentality of Charlotte and Emily Brontë a fresh analytical
talent.

DOUGHTY, Charles M.

PASSAGES FROM ARABIA DESERTA. Selected
by EDWARD GARNETT. With a Frontispiece   *No. 21*

'Charles Montagu Doughty was one of the great men of our
day, the author of a unique prose masterpiece. For many
readers it is a book so majestic, so vital, of such incomparable
beauty of thought, of observation, and of diction as to occupy
a place apart among their most cherished literary possessions.'
Observer

GRAVES, Robert

GOOD-BYE TO ALL THAT. With eight illustrations *No. 22*

'*Good-bye to all That* is a very good book, both picturesque
and honest, and excellently written. Robert Graves is a fine
poet—none better to-day, in my view. All poets write good
prose, and he does. . . . It is the sincere and convincing
expression of a distinguished individuality.' ARNOLD BENNETT

HENDY, E. W.

WILD EXMOOR THROUGH THE YEAR   *No. 37*

'Mr. Hendy is one of the best writers among our naturalists,
with abundant and intimate knowledge of his country and its
wild inhabitants. There must be many people who will find
this their book; now that we have lost our old freedom of
passage across country, with the rights of way curtailed or
quietly filched almost everywhere, Exmoor and Dartmoor
mean more than ever.' EDWARD THOMPSON in *The Observer*

HINDUS, Maurice

HUMANITY UPROOTED   *No. 41*

'I have just read your book. It answers a score of questions I've
been asking about Russia and a score of others I should have
asked had I known enough to ask them. It is as illuminating
and exciting as it is convincing. I've learnt more from it than
I have from any other book I've read for years.' *From a letter
to the author by* MR. H. G. WELLS

HORN, Alfred Aloysius

TRADER HORN (The Ivory Coast in the Earlies).
Edited by ETHELREDA LEWIS. With an Introduction
by JOHN GALSWORTHY. Illustrated with portraits   *No.* 4

'This is a gorgeous book, more full of sheer stingo than any
you are likely to come across in a day's march among the book-
shops of wherever you may be.' *From* MR. JOHN GALSWORTHY'S
Introduction

THE WATERS OF AFRICA. Edited by
ETHELREDA LEWIS   *No.* 28

Even more mysterious than the cannibals and shadowy rivers
of Western Africa is the East Coast of fifty years ago with its
magic island of Madagascar and its island-sewn Mozambique
Channel. Here, as in his other book, the famous conversations
of Horn with his editor amplify the old man's narrative.

JACKSON, Holbrook

THE EIGHTEEN NINETIES. With twenty-six
illustrations   *No.* 17

'The curious investigator of the future will always be able to
see the period's main outlines, and to find them clearly traced
in Mr. Holbrook Jackson's animated and attractive pages.'
The Daily Telegraph

LANGDON-DAVIES, John

A SHORT HISTORY OF WOMEN   *No.* 42

A most readable and reasonable book in which the author
traces the ideas and theories which have been held about the
position of women and the treatment which has been meted out
to them during the last six thousand years.

LEYEL, Mrs. C. F.

THE MAGIC OF HERBS   *No.* 34

'Mrs. Leyel has gone deep into her subject and has brought
back wonders from the earliest dawn of science and from all
parts of the world . . . treasures of curious and useful informa-
tion purged of their dross are presented, not too methodically
and yet methodically enough.' *Manchester Guardian*

LUBBOCK, Percy

EARLHAM. With a Frontispiece   *No.* 7

'The book seems too intimate to be reviewed. We want to be
allowed to read it, and to dream over it, and keep silence about
it. His judgment is perfect, his humour is true and ready;
his touch light and prim; his prose is exact and clean and full
of music.' *Times*

SHADES OF ETON   *No.* 30

The author was at Eton in the 'nineties of the last century. To
those years belong the figures and scenes recalled in this book—
in which they appear as they seemed to a boy, and in which an
attempt is made to measure the effect of Eton on a boy's
imagination. Warre himself, F. W. Warre-Cornish and his
wife, H. E. Luxmoore and A. C. Benson were among those
who counted most deeply in that impression; these and other
figures familiar to Etonians of that time are sketched in detail.

LUDWIG, Emil

GENIUS AND CHARACTER. Illustrated by six-
teen portraits   *No.* 9

'As in his longer biographies, it is the dramatic values of motive
and action he seeks, the flashes of illumination in the chiaroscuro
investing a lonely figure. This is not a ponderous book; it is a
series of vivacious and sometimes very moving studies.' *The
Spectator*

MAYO, Katherine

MOTHER INDIA. Illustrated   *No.* 5

'It is certainly the most fascinating, the most devastating, and at
the same time the most important and truthful book that has
been written about India for a good deal more than a generation.' *New Statesman*

McCURDY, Edward

THE MIND OF LEONARDO DA VINCI   *No.* 31

Mr. McCurdy has made a special study of the manuscript and
notebooks of Leonardo, a selection of which he edited. He
attempts here a biographical study of Leonardo in which the
subject's mind and mentality is the selective factor. The book
is in three parts and deals with the period of his life at Florence,
at Milan, and during the years of his wandering.

MUIR, Edwin

JOHN KNOX. Illustrated by four portraits   *No.* 12

The study is not concerned with the truth or the falsehood of Calvinism, but rather presents the Calvinist in all his activities from the greatest to the most trifling, and shows his creed working out, here in heroic and there in ridiculous form.

MURRY, J. Middleton

SON OF WOMAN   *No.* 40

'A very detailed exposition of the life-work of D. H. Lawrence, and it would be impossible—I will say that—to find a better interpretation. It will be indispensable to any future historian of this prophetic period: Mr. Murry was a great friend of Lawrence, and is excellently placed to tell us exactly the significance of every fresh development in this gospel.' WYNDHAM LEWIS in *Time and Tide*

NILES, Blair

CONDEMNED TO DEVIL'S ISLAND. The biography of a French Convict. Illustrated from drawings by B. K. MORRIS   *No.* 10

Mrs. Blair Niles is the first woman to have been allowed to visit the most notorious Devil's Island since it became a penal colony. She describes this penal settlement in the person of a young French burglar, and tells an almost unbearable tale of thousands of men starved of hope and leisure.

POWYS, John Cowper

THE MEANING OF CULTURE   *No.* 33

'Here in a dozen chapters of eloquent and glowing prose, Mr. Powys describes for every reader that citadel which is himself and explains to him how it may be strengthened and upheld and on what terms it is most worth upholding.' *Manchester Guardian*

RANSOME, Arthur

ROD AND LINE   *No.* 38

'*Rod and Line* must be placed in the front rank of contemporary angling literature, both for its insight into the "sunset hues" through which most of us see our sport (in reminiscence), and for its literary excellence. It possesses, too, just that touch of whimsical humour with which most of us (again in reminiscence) clothe the nakedness of those distressing times which confirm us in our conviction that Job was no fisherman.' *Field*

READ, Herbert

WORDSWORTH No. 35

'This study of Wordsworth is to me a landmark in English criticism such as we have not had since the *Biographia Literaria*. . . . If ever I recognized great work, proclaimed by its own strength and simplicity, here is such.' RICHARD CHURCH in the *Spectator*

SHAND, P. Morton

A BOOK OF FOOD No. 8

Dr. Johnson said: 'Most people have a foolish way of not minding, or pretending not to mind, what they eat. For my own part I mind my belly most studiously and very carefully; for I look upon it that he who does not mind his belly will hardly mind anything else.'

SIEGFRIED, André

AMERICA COMES OF AGE. A French Analysis.
Illustrated by eight maps and diagrams. Translated from the French by H. H. HEMMING and DORIS HEMMING No. 1

'It is a brilliant study of the most important, and in some ways the most interesting, though certainly not the loveliest, nation on earth.' THE VERY REV. DEAN W. R. INGE

SULLIVAN, J. W. N.

BEETHOVEN, His spiritual development. Illustrated No. 15

'Few men are better qualified to write a study of Beethoven than Mr. J. W. N. Sullivan. . . .' *The Spectator*
'It is a striking merit of Mr. Sullivan's book that it explains Beethoven to the unmusical philosopher.' *The New Statesman*

TAYLOR, G. R. Stirling

SEVEN NINETEENTH-CENTURY STATESMEN No. 39

'This vivid book . . . has the virtues of penetration, skilful arrangement, clear purpose, a lively style. It makes an excellent summary of the political history of England during most of the nineteenth century . . . it has not a dull page; the author has a keen eye for character, and an enviable gift for presentation.' OSBERT BURDETT in the *Observer*

WALLAS, Graham
THE ART OF THOUGHT *No.* 24
A book written with the practical purpose of helping the apprentice thinker to become a competent craftsman. The author examines the proposition that the human mind is 'actuated by instinct, but instrumented by reason,' and suggests its application to our own thought.

WEST, Rebecca
THE STRANGE NECESSITY: Critical Essays *No.* 18
Miss Rebecca West's book is a sequence of challenging studies of modern books and authors. *The Strange Necessity*—Art—which is so inclusive of opposites. Speculating on this brings Miss West to an analysis of literature, and the discovery of a double and vital function which it fulfils for man.

WILLIAMS-ELLIS, Clough & Amabel
THE PLEASURES OF ARCHITECTURE.
Illustrated from drawings and photographs *No.* 14
This book will bring enlightenment and entertainment to those who like a well-built house or office building when they see it, but are not quite sure as to the reasons why they like it.

WOOLLEY, C. L.
DEAD TOWNS AND LIVING MEN *No.* 29
Dead Towns and Living Men describes the training that goes to make a fully equipped archæologist, the sort of places, usually far away from the beaten track, that he lives in, and the sort of men, usually ignorant and sometimes half-civilised, whom he must control and live with. Archæology as a satisfying human adventure has never been better described than in this book.

WRIGHT, Eugene
THE GREAT HORN SPOON *No.* 36
'In *The Great Horn Spoon* a young American has presented us with a travel book that is really worth reading . . . it is alive . . . he writes with gusto, he carries us along with him, makes us feel hot and cold, fearful or exultant, conjures up jungles and deserts for us.' J. B. PRIESTLEY

THE NOVELS OF RADCLYFFE HALL, uniform
edition. Small cr. 8vo. Black cloth, fully gilt. 5s. net
a volume.

THE UNLIT LAMP
ADAM'S BREED

THE NOVELS OF SINCLAIR LEWIS, Nobel Prize
edition. Mr. Sinclair Lewis was awarded the Nobel Prize
for literature in 1930. Uniform edition. Small cr. 8vo.
Red cloth, fully gilt. 5s. net a volume.

BABBITT
THE JOB
MAIN STREET
OUR MR. WRENN
MARTIN ARROWSMITH
FREE AIR
DODSWORTH
ELMER GANTRY
THE TRAIL OF THE HAWK

THE COLLECTED WORKS OF MARY WEBB,
uniform edition. Small cr. 8vo. Green cloth, fully gilt.
5s. net a volume.

GONE TO EARTH. With an Introduction by JOHN BUCHAN

SEVEN FOR A SECRET. With an Introduction by ROBERT
LYND

PRECIOUS BANE. With an Introduction by the RT. HON.
STANLEY BALDWIN

THE GOLDEN ARROW. With an Introduction by G. K.
CHESTERTON

THE HOUSE IN DORMER FOREST. With an Introduction
by the REV. H. R. L. SHEPPARD

POEMS AND THE SPRING OF JOY. With an Introduction
by WALTER DE LA MARE

ARMOUR WHEREIN HE TRUSTED. A Collection of her
short stories, including the unfinished novel upon which she
was working at the time of her death. With an Introduction by
MARTIN ARMSTRONG

THE NOVELS OF MISS E. H. YOUNG, uniform edition. Small cr. 8vo. Blue cloth, fully gilt. 5s. net a volume.

WILLIAM
THE MISSES MALLETT
YONDER
THE VICAR'S DAUGHTER
MOOR FIRES
MISS MOLE

THE PLAYS OF EUGENE O'NEILL, uniform edition. Blue cloth, gilt. Cr. 8vo. 7s. 6d. net a volume.

THE EMPEROR JONES: and other Plays. *The Emperor Jones, The Straw,* and *Diff'rent*

THE MOON OF THE CARIBBEES: and other Plays of the Sea. *The Moon of the Caribbees, Bound East for Cardiff, The Long Voyage Home, In the Zone, Ile, Where the Cross is Made,* and *The Rope.* With an Introduction by ST. JOHN ERVINE

THE HAIRY APE: and other Plays. *The Hairy Ape, Anna Christie, The First Man*

BEYOND THE HORIZON. Two Plays. *Beyond the Horizon* and *Gold*

ALL GOD'S CHILLUN GOT WINGS. Three Plays. Including *Desire Under the Elms* and *Welded*

THE GREAT GOD BROWN and other Plays. *The Great God Brown, The Fountain, Before Breakfast* and *The Dreamy Kid*

STRANGE INTERLUDE. A Play in Nine Acts

LAZARUS LAUGHED and DYNAMO

MARCO MILLIONS. A Play in Three Acts. 5s. net

MOURNING BECOMES ELECTRA. A Trilogy. *Homecoming. The Hunted. The Haunted*

ALPHABETICAL INDEX TO TITLES

(In this index, volumes in both 'The Travellers' Library' and 'The Life and Letters Series' are included, as well as volumes in the 'Collected Works.')

46

48

THE TRAVELLERS' LIBRARY

NUMERICAL INDEX TO TITLES

THE LIFE AND LETTERS SERIES

NUMERICAL INDEX TO TITLES

Made and printed in Gt. Britain by The Garden City Press Ltd., Letchworth and London